"Gail Hagan has been a wonderful spiritual guidance counselor in my life. She has guided me through a divorce, death of my mother and also depression. These would have been some of the toughest situations to deal with, if it was not for the spiritual solutions Gail Hagan taught me. This is an inspiring story of triumph through an awful way of growing up, to being chosen to spread messages from the spirit world. This story will inspire you to move forward in your own trying times along with incurring prosperity within. This book can and will inspire you to overcome obstacles that seem utterly impossible to endure. Some techniques that the author has explained will guide you into becoming a better listener, and to better understand how to apply the spirit guide teachings and overall become a better individual. The author has shared personal information that she has endured throughout her life, along with learning how to apply the spiritual solutions to her problems."

Ronda Antonelli

are you, *You?*

how to cope with the haunting memories of abuse

are you, *You?*

TATE PUBLISHING & *Enterprises*

Published by Tate Publishing & Enterprises, LLC
127 E. Trade Center Terrace | Mustang, Oklahoma 73064 USA
1.888.361.9473 | www.tatepublishing.com

Tate Publishing is committed to excellence in the publishing industry. The company reflects the philosophy established by the founders, based on Psalms 68:11,
"The Lord gave the word and great was the company of those who published it."

Book design copyright © 2007 by Tate Publishing, LLC. All rights reserved.
Cover design by Janae Glass
Interior design by Jennifer Redden

Published in the United States of America

ISBN: 978-1-6024731-4-X
07.05.02

Table of Contents

Listen

I have found it very amazing that there are so many individuals that in actuality do not know who they are. Oh yes, they state their names, but who are they/you? I have learned many things in my life time so far, and it even amazes me today what I have actually applied to what I have learned. My book starts out describing my life during the time of living at home. What was I to have learned during that time frame? I hope to be able to answer that question one day. As you will read from my story of a child, I am very thankful though that the laws have changed for the better in regards to protecting the young and the innocent. It does not seem to me that there were any laws for the young or the innocent during the early years of my life. I know that there are so many individuals out there that have gone through some of the similar things that I have. Remember everyone, you have to know who you are, be true to yourself because you always have to come back to you. Think about it, after you have perhaps allowed someone to take advantage of you and then you get all disgusted with yourself after you had realized what you had just did. You then go back to your thoughts and think and think and think over and over and over what you just went through. So now you are back with yourself, alone and feel somewhat stupid about what you had just been through. It is such a great shame that many of us have now become adults and do not really know who we are; however, I hope that something that I have written in the following pages will help at least one of you become you and know who you are. I have not discussed all of my life because basically it was a mess and I do not remember it all. However, I did state some things that I had gone through in hopes that one of you readers that has also gone through a lot of negatives know that your garbage has happened in the past and you need to quit letting the past negative stuff run and ruin your life today. Have you ever heard of 'spiritual warfare'? Christians know about spiritual warfare but they still allow past negatives to ruin their present day lives.

For many years I have talked with and heard many people discuss their negatives. Whether the negatives are of poor health or how someone had ripped them off. I have read in the Bible that you are to speak as if it has already happened. That means that if you continually talk about the past negatives and do not release them then actually you are claiming them for the rest of your doomed days on this earth and the past negatives will run and ruin your life. If you know that the stuff did happen, you had gone through all that negative stuff and today the negatives are not happening and you had made it through all of that mess of *whatever kind*, than speak as if you are well and happy. A great saying that I have used for years is "what you think, you speak, you get." It is believed by many that when you learn of, gather knowledge of, and have some type of spiritual experience(s) than you are a much more of a part of the cosmic energies. All of us are of spirit and human form however there still are many that have no knowledge of the psychic/spiritual. Can you imagine that there are individuals that do not know what the psychic/spiritual realm is about? So after you gather some of any psychic/spiritual knowledge/information you have to hold stronger onto positive thoughts and energy because you will have a much stronger spiritual warfare against you. The reason for that is because spiritual warfare is of a negative spiritual source. The enemy of Christians is the devil which is the spiritual warfare; the devil does not want anyone, whether Christian or not, to be doing anything that is positive. The devil and/or enemy is the spiritual warfare; the fight is against principalities and not against human beings around you. You are fighting against other individual's hang-ups, their insecurities, and negatives not actually against the human unless the negatives really get out of hand and the physical abuse gets involved.

As you will soon learn, I have had a difficult life so far. Many times I have asked myself, was I really a horrible person perhaps in a past life that I need to learn many things during this life? I totally believe that each one of us is here on earth to learn something. I have not been to heaven and back so I actually do not know how it all works. However, from what I have learned so far I do believe that we do indeed need to learn something from our each daily walks here on earth. I do watch what I speak, think, and feel. When a negative anything gets into my thoughts I diligently get a positive impression immediately to my thoughts so that I do not have such a horrible spiritual warfare going on. I will always have a spiritual warfare going on because as I already stated, I work on saying positive things to others. I work diligently on being a positive vessel and human influence for others around me. It is as if the spiritual warfare does not want you to succeed in a positive manner. Perhaps if you were to cheat or hurt another individual then you will not have such a spiritual warfare. However, there are those that believe that there is a higher power and to those individuals the spiritual warfare will be rough on you. The Bible is like a guidance for all people that are working daily to do positive things and it is also the history of what others had done in their lives before our time. I believe that most of the written things are there to try and give me hope to get through my negative messes if I had chosen to go into a negative mess/situation. There are many non-believers of a higher human power, such as a teacher or a therapist, that do not believe how I and many others do, and you know what? That is their prerogative to think that way. A very long time ago I had the same beliefs until one day when I was born again.

Child Abuse

I grew up in an abusive home. I was raised in an unloving and uncaring family environment. There were no hugs or family kisses given out nor were there any positive words said toward myself or towards my siblings that I had seen, felt or heard. Everyday was a struggle just to do the appropriate things that my parents and/or the adults around wanted me to do. It seemed as though everything that I had done was wrong by my parent's or the adult's standards. My parents were always saying negative statements about the way that I had talked, dressed, and even the way that I handled each of my daily duties. It seemed as though every time they had seen me in their presence they would cuss me out. They would call me *retarded slut, little b——-ch* and *moron*—just to name a *few* things that they had called me. Now I was too young to even know what those words meant, but because they had said it and in the way that they had said it, I figured that they must not be good words. They would call all of us girls, *the little bitches*. Again, I did not know what that meant either. Today I can comprehend and say that because of this negative environment that I was being raised in I did not realize that I was being taught how to sin and/or how to hate and distrust others. Sin is meant in a way that I had learned to harm others, to talk at and to do to others the same way that the adults had talked and done to me. At the time I did not understand why I had to go through such awful situations, but now I believe I know that from each sinful situation, I have gained an abundance of knowledge that has made me stronger to go through other situations that might not be of a sinful nature or as hard to deal with. At that time and for a long time I had believed that I knew how to deal with others. First of all, you do not trust anyone because if you do than certainly someone will hurt you really bad. Second, they will take all of your money and or material items. Or perhaps you have feelings for someone and you believe that they also have feelings for you when in actuality they only have feelings for what they can take from you or how they can hurt you.

The next few paragraphs are a few things that I do remember while growing up. I do not remember very much; maybe because most of it was too horrible to remember. I have some great people around me now and then that had helped me a lot of what I had gone through and some of them had told me the things that I did not remember. I have also stated some of my information from grade to grade because it was easier to remember it that way.

I have two sisters and two brothers; however, Jean, my birth mom, had more than eight pregnancies which only five of them had survived. From looking at each one of us and what I had heard through the years, it seems as though we have several different fathers. Bobby, the oldest, was born in the month of April and does look like Robert Sr., Jan, born the month of July and Glen, born in the month of May, look alike; however neither of them look like Robert Sr., Joanne, born the month of February, does not look like any of us and I, born the month of January, do have a cleft on my chin like Robert Sr. does; however, that does not mean that I am his flesh and blood. I didn't know where my mom had gone to until years later when I was approximately sixteen. I had heard that Jean had met a guy at work and married him. As far as I can remember, only one man, named Cliff, had always been around. One time I remember that both of them had taken me for a ride in his red convertible with the top down. The wind was blowing really hard and Jean's head scarf had come off of her head and blew over my head, over the back of the car and out to the distance and we all laughed. I have seen pictures of myself with Jean and Cliff, but I do not remember the situations happening. My dad, Robert Sr. had been a truck driver for as long as I can remember and Jean was a secretary at his company, so basically, they had worked together. I do not remember my parents being around much before they had gotten divorced, but I had thought we were all happy. Robert Sr. must have been working a lot of hours because I do not remember many good times while being with him or him being around a lot. Since they had gotten divorced Robert Sr. had the obligation of raising all five of us kids without Jean; however, he did have several individuals there to help him watch us. Basically, I had thought he did a great job of keeping us together until later in my life when I started to realize that I was not raised in a normal household. There was at first a babysitter that would come after school some nights while they were still married and make us brown sugar cooked in butter that we, my siblings and I, had thought was a great treat. Later times he would have other females there to help watch us.

We all lived in a duplex in the city of Hometown, Illinois. My sisters and I shared the same room. I had the top bunk, Janet had the bottom bunk, and Joanne had a separate bed. One morning while lying on the top bunk, I saw a hand with brass knuckles outside my bedroom window. I had gotten scared and covered up my head with the blankets. It had snowed that night so when I had gotten up out of bed and got dressed the next morning, I went outside by my bedroom window to see if there were any shoe tracks in the snow because I had figured if I seen the brass knuckles and it had snowed, than there should be some foot prints. There were no shoe prints in the snow, which had caused me some confusion because I know that I did see those brass knuckles at the window. We did not have any curtains or blinds on our windows so when the sun rose, so did I because the room had become so bright, especially sleeping on the top bunk. My two brothers, Bobby and Glen, slept somewhere else in the house in another room. I do not remember ever seeing their bedroom.

In our front room we had a bay window with curtains on the front side of it. Bobby would get my mom's large bra, a D cup, I believe, put it on, stand behind the drapes in front of the open window and do a dance for us other four. He was so funny and we would laugh so hard. I think he had gotten into trouble for doing that, because he did not do that anymore. One year for Christmas, Grampa Billy had made Janet, Joanne and I each a baby doll cradle. We girls also got a hand muff, it was a white fluffy thing that had a space in the sides that we put our hands into. I only knew this because I had seen a picture of us with those. I remember one day, my sisters and I had been all dressed up in a light pink jacket and matching hat. I really do not remember how it happened, but I was told that I had pushed my sister Jo down into the muddy water and I got into big trouble. Jan had said that she and I were caught smoking behind the church and we tried to burn the bushes outside next to the church. We had a green car with no back seat. Everywhere we would go, us five kids would have to stand up or sit on the floor in the back—no seat car, and I had hated that green car. One day, we were left in the car by ourselves with an ash tray full of cigarette butts. One of us started lighting the old butts and burning the material on the roof of that old green car. The material no longer was attached to the roof of the car and it had hung over the drivers head. Not long after that, I remember driving in a rambler that had a lot of seats. One day Bobby and I were playing in the driveway when he hit me in the head with a steel rake. I was wearing a red hat. My head had hurt really badly and we went in and told Jean what had happened, she took off my red hat and it was full of blood. I guess I was okay because I do not know what happened to me next.

The streets where we had lived in Hometown, Illinois use to flood all the time when it would rain really heavy. I remember many people would have their row boats out on the street giving everyone rides up and down the roads. To this day I still think that was a great high light to living in that duplex. I now remember that I use to hear voices on the other side of the wall because the walls were that thin. How cool was that? We could listen to the neighbors talking and yelling. One day, Bobby went off on his bike and I had run after him. He kept telling me to go home but I did not listen. He then left me and kept going and I remember starting to cry. A really nice lady came to me and had asked me if I was lost and I said, *yes.* Somehow I was back at home.

Another House

I remember one day we were at another house, which we moved here with only Robert Sr. I must have been in second grade at the time. Shortly after we moved to this new home on Sayre Street there basically were no adults there except for Robert Sr. once in awhile. My sister Jan would do all the cooking and she would make our breakfast. I remember eating farina that had to be cooked. After she was done cooking it, it was not thoroughly cooked and some of the dry stuff would get onto the spoon and we still had to eat it. Jan also had to do all the other cooking, such as mashed lumpy potatoes and lumpy gravy made with flour and water and meat grease, which actually wasn't too bad once you had gotten use to it. Janet was not very tall but she had a mighty temper. I think she really kept us all in line such as behaving, taking baths, no fighting, getting our homework done and whatever else that a sister-mom had to take care of. She would have to wash the dishes, which she could hardly reach over the tub sink to reach the dishes. The tub sink was actually a sink in the utility room where the water from the washing machine would empty into. I think Bobby was twelve years old, Janet was eight years old, I had to be seven years old, Joanne was six years old, and Glen was two years old. I do remember Bobby getting into a lot of trouble all the time. Maybe one reason was because he never stayed home and babysat us.

The home on Sayre Street had a very large back yard. I do remember that way in the back of the yard was a chicken coop that housed many ducks. Several times a week, I would have to go out and clean all the ducks mess up from the coops' wooden floor. Those ducks really made some nasty messes inside the coop. During the winter season, I would also have to clean the coop. All of the ducks water would be dumped onto the floor. Since the ducks had made such a nasty mess anyways, the water had frozen over the mess. I would have to chop, scrape and loosen up whatever I could until the coops floor was basically cleaned. There were a few male ducks that were very mean. They would attack me when I would have to go near them. Every time I went by them, either to feed them, clean up their coop or to just walk near them, they would attack my ankles. I was a scrawny, skinny little girl and had no meat on my ankles. I was so afraid when I had to go out there, however, I was more afraid of my dad, so I went out and cleaned the coop. I did not have any boots that fit me so I had to use some adults boots that were way to big for me. When I would try to run from the ducks, I would trip and fall and then the male ducks would also attack other parts of my body. The female ducks were quite friendly, however, the male ducks would make sure that no one would or could go near them. The ducks would lay eggs and I would have to go out there and retrieve them so we could have eggs to eat. The male ducks did not like that and during and after the collection of the eggs, they would hurt every part of my body that they could reach. I would cry and cry and tell my dad what the ducks were doing, but he said just do the job and quit being a cry baby. So I did.

The neighbors next to our home on Sayre Street seemed to be descent individuals. I remember there was a grandmother, her daughter, the daughter's husband, and two boys. They were always nice to us. When it was cold out and we couldn't go into our house, they let us go into their house. The adults in my house use to talk badly about them, but, I could not figure out why because they were nicer to me than my parents were. One day I had gone over to the neighbors' house and they served me a hot cup of tea. The grandmother used to carefully press her teabag on the inside of her full cup of tea. So one day I had thought that I could also do that her way. The cup of hot tea had spilled all over my chest and my shirt was stuck onto my chest. The grandmother had grabbed me, threw cold water on my chest, pulled my shirt up over my head, and off of me. They had put something on my chest to help with the burning. I can barely see the burn to this day. One of the boys had made our house members very angry, so we children had thrown eggs all over the side of their house. The siding that they had on their house, had been rough, scratchy, an ugly green color, and old. I remember Janet, Bobby and I had to wash the side of their house, which was not easy, and we did not get it very clean. After we had done our best, my dad had his turn with our bodies. Yes and don't you all know how that felt. To this day, I feel badly about egging their house because they were the best people that I had known as a kid growing up. My little brother, Glen, was very young and such a cutie. Because of the way that the months had fallen with school starting in September, all of us would be an older age by the time we had started school. I had to be in second grade, and eight years old. Jo was a year younger than me and Jan a year older. All three of us were in grade school. My dad used to always say that I better not hear that any of you had stayed home from school.

Housekeeper and Other Adults

Did I mention the house keeper yet, maybe not? It seemed to be not long after we had moved to the house on Sayre St that there was a different lady there. She was medium tall, heavy set, short curly hair, she wore glasses and she drank a lot. We were told that she was the housekeeper, Franny. It seemed like every couple of weeks an ambulance would come to the house and pick her up and take her away. I never heard or remember hearing my dad and her fighting; however, I do remember some days that she would use funny faces at him. But that is how all that went and it was none of our business as we were told. On different days, I had found this out after I had left home, she (the housekeeper) would take each one of us four kids, one at a time, to her male friends house. We were not to tell our dad what we did that day because Franny, the housekeeper, said that our dad would beat her and our backsides. So we never told him. When the report cards came out, Franny had told him some lies about why we had so many days off of school. One day there was no babysitter for Glen and someone was supposed to watch him. I do not know where Franny was, but I guess that was not my dad's problem. All three of us had a real dilemma. How were we going to watch Glen, yet go to school? Well, we had asked one of the neighbors to watch him, which we thought was a great idea. After my dad had gotten home, he had busted our bottoms big time with his usual black belt or he would beat us with his 2 x 4. He use to leave these horrible red welts all over our bodies after he was done beating us with that black belt and even bigger red and black welts after he use to hit us with his wooden pieces of thick 2 x 4's. From what I gather today about back then, the neighbor had brought Glen home and had a long discussion with my dad. Robert Sr. did not like nor allow anyone to tell him what he had better be doing about his own personal situations.

Franny used to make good egg sandwiches, but after I watched her eat one, it made me really sick to my stomach. She would take a bite of her egg sandwich and chew some and then stick her finger in her mouth. It was so sickening to watch her, that every time I eat an egg sandwich now, which is not often, I can see her eating hers. I remember one time she and I had taken a taxi cab to some house that had a lot of back stairs that seemed to go on forever. I would have to sit on the porch outside the back door which seemed to be for hours. After that time I do remember the ambulance coming by and getting her. One day all of us kids must have gotten her really mad, because my dad had gotten home when it was really dark out and he had come upstairs while we were all sleeping and turned the light on and woke us up. He started beating all of us with a 2 x 4. I tell you what, that board really hurt. He had broke it over my back, almost broke my sister Jan's arm with it and the rest of the kids, I don't remember how bad they got it. I remember that while he would beat us we all each in our own turn would dance around him in a circle trying to get away from his right hand. He would hold us so tightly with his left hand as he beat us with the board in his right hand. I know that there was a whole lot a crying up there that night. Franny would make sure that we ate oatmeal for breakfast and then would not be allowed in the house until dinner time. Dinner usually consisted of mashed potatoes and cream corn. I do remember that we would have to stay outside even if we have to go to the bathroom or we were cold or even hungry. The neighbors would give us some food and sometimes we could go into their house if we were too cold. Basically, I only remember about my younger years as being beat up. I did have a few nice individuals around me that had tried to help me out; however, those nasty, mean people always had the upper hand where I had been concerned. I do not remember much about my childhood except what I had already mentioned previously. There were times in my childhood that I was so afraid of my dad that I would wet my pants. If he would look at me in a certain way, I would wet my pants. If he would talk to me in a certain way, I would wet my pants. Basically, I was so afraid of him that I would naturally wet my pants when he was near me and then he would whip my butt for wetting my pants.

The housekeeper was drunk most of the time. She had her hair curled up in a 1950s style that did not help her looks any. I believe that she always had really short finger nails and only wore red nail polish that she had chewed most of it off. From what I can remember, I think she always tried to get into my dad's bed and things didn't work out and then an ambulance would show up. A few days later she would return. What was I to learn from her? I think it was to not wear chipped red nail polish. Also I feel that it was to learn how to eat food. You definitely would not keep your fingers in your mouth while chewing your food. Well, think about it. You are chewing your food with your finger in your mouth and the food is falling out of your mouth. As I had already stated, I still love a great egg and mayo sandwich, I just try very diligently not to have her face in my mind while I am eating one. She was okay for a housekeeper. She didn't hit us or nothing bad that I can remember. One day she came home from the hairdressers and they found lice in her hair. Of course, she combed our hair with her brush. That evening, we had our hair soaked in kerosene, wrapped over with a towel for hours. That stuff burned my ears and neck really badly. Boy oh boy did that stuff stink. She had the lice but she did not have any kerosene put on her head. As I sit here and try to remember my life as a child, I do find it quite difficult and the memories are quite painful. One great thing that I do remember is basically what we kids had done wrong during the day, either she did not tell Robert Sr. or she told it in a way that did not seem to be too bad. Because I really do not remember having many beatings while she was around. So I guess I was really depressed when she was not there anymore.

We did not get or own any bicycles. One day I had found a bike in the trash that had worked. I was riding the bike, and then decided to let go of the handle bars. I was going fairly fast and shortly after letting go of the handle bars I had fallen very hard on my face onto the side walk. I was all cut up, bleeding and crying hysterically. I do not remember how I had gotten home. After I did get home, the housekeeper had washed me up some and put me to bed. The grandmother from next door had come over to see how I was doing, and got very upset when she had found out that I was in bed sleeping because she had thought that I may have had a concussion. I remember her yelling at the housekeeper telling her to put me onto the couch and not to let me sleep, and to put ice on me. She listened and I am here today to talk about it. My brother Bob wasn't around much while she was there. I really don't remember him being around much at all when I was young. I didn't remember seeing him for a long time and then never again. Later years I had found out that he had joined the service. I guess he did get into a lot of trouble and that was one of the best ways to keep him safe.

I always would wet my pants because I would get cold and have to urinate. I remember that I would have to go to the bathroom a lot but there was no bathroom available for me to use. I was also afraid to use the bathroom in my house because we were told not to come in until we were called in. At night I was afraid to go to the bathroom because if my dad had to get in the bathroom and we kids were in there he would get really angry at us. So I guess basically when he needed to use the bathroom it had better be available for him at his beck and call. All of us kids, except Glen, I don't know where he was after the one time having the neighbor watch him, had a light jacket to wear in the winter time. We had no hats, no gloves and no boots, neither in the winter nor on a rainy day. We were fed breakfast before we left for school, we had no lunch to take with us and had dinner late in the evening. We ran almost all the way to school on those cold days, which I was told was more than a mile, just so that we could get warm. I would be so cold that one time I had cried and the tears had frozen on my face. I believe that each one of us had to learn how to deal with being cold. Jan's hands would get so chapped, bloody, and they would hurt her so badly. My skin would always be so red and would hurt to the touch. Some days the air would be so cold that a little breeze would get into my ears and I would get a horrible earache, but I was not allowed to complain nor cry. Jo would just stand there so sweet looking, freezing her little self.

We did have two choices on the directions that we could go

to school, which we had called one way the long way and the other the short way. The long way meant that we would go from our house to the end of the block and head to the left. The walk was very long. We would go past one block, which this was not a city block it was a country block. Then we had to go through this horrid field. I never liked going through it when it had started to get dark because the grass was higher than I was and it had felt really freaky when I would walk on the beaten down grass and mud that we had used as a pathway. On one side of us while we were walking was a small creek that ran along the road and on the other side of that creek was a fence that was not too sturdy. That fence was very difficult to climb. It could have been twelve feet high and when one would try to climb it, it would constantly move in and out where you would literally fall in and out and then off the fence into the watered creek just below that area. So that fence was not an option to climb to get to school. When we got to the end of the fence we would turn the corner to the right, go a few feet, make another right and now we had side-walks to walk on. The walk to there was not even the half way mark to Lieb elementary school that we were going to. Now that we had made it to the sidewalk we would have to walk all the way back to our street, on the other side of the fence, and then walk another six to ten city blocks until we came to the end of that street. Then we would turn left and go another four blocks to the school grounds. I believe that we had left at 8:00 am and sometimes were still late for school and believe me we did not monkey around on the way to school. The short cut that we sometimes would take to school was not too bad on sunny days. If it had recently rained and/or was raining we did not want to go that road unless we had left for school later than 8:00 am. From the end of our street we would turn to the right. There was no road there, just dirt and a little bit of a grass field. There was the rest of the fence that had been along this side also with the continuous of the creek. When the dirt had gotten wet, it would become a slip and slide situation during our walk to school. I am not sure how long of a walk it was, but I believe it was six to ten city blocks to the end of the fence and to the dreaded creek. There were some large stones in the water that if you figured correctly and made the precise jump, you could get through the creek with little difficulty or so my brother did. I am in second grade, Joanne was in first, Janet was in third and I believe Bobby must have been in the sixth grade. I never liked going that way because I would always miss the rocks and would get wet and muddy. The floor of the creek was mainly quicksand when it had water in it. I remember one time Bobby had jumped over and missed the rocks and he landed in the quicksand and started to sink. We girls did our best to help him out, we did succeed, but what a muddy mess we were. After all of us had gotten across the creek we straightened up ourselves the best that we could and went on to school. Would you believe that the school had called our house and told on us? Yes, indeed, there was a lot of singing going on in that attic that evening. After that incident we were told to never go that way again. We still went that way but not on a muddy day.

Third Grade

My two sisters and I had slept on one side of the upstairs while my two brothers had slept on the other side. There was nothing fancy about where we slept. It had open rafters, a wooded floor, and if you did not pick up your feet while you were walking you would get slivers. One sliver was enough for me, because it was really deep in my foot. I called these bedrooms the attic. Some of the insulation was becoming loose from between the wood. There was also a live electrical wire that hung down from the ceiling. You know those microphones that hung down from above one of the singers on television in the late 1950's. That is what I had thought and we were lucky to have one in our bedrooms. Anyways, one bad rainy day, my brothers and sisters and I were all playing in the attic. We were playing, running and yelling and carrying on and having a great time. On the boys side of the room I had seen that microphone hanging from the ceiling and I wanted to talk and sing into it. I had gotten a hold of it and could not let go. I was told that I looked like I was doing the Irish jig. My brother Bobby had grabbed a pair of his jeans and came charging at me and knocked me off of the live wire. At first he scared me because of the way he was running at me but then I was very glad, because I was loose from all of the funny feeling stuff. I was sitting on one of the beds and my whole body, especially my right leg kept shaking really badly. My dad later said that he didn't come up sooner because he had thought that we were just rough playing. They did not take me to the doctors. I remember crying a lot and then was outside sitting on a swing in the backyard holding my right- hand wrist. My right hand thumb and part of that hand was burnt. Would you believe that one of the adults had gotten me a bucket and put it next to my bed so that if I had to go potty I could use it? I had that bucket by the side of my bed so that if I had to go to the bathroom I could go in it which I guess on some nights I actually did use it. I did have some urine in it and during the night my hand was hurting really bad. I had put my hand in the cold urine and it made it feel much better. By the next morning, my hand had a big puss sack over my thumb from the end of my finger nail to the end of my thumb by my wrist. They had to take me to the doctors this time because I was missing school and they could not send me to school with my thumb in such a mess. I was in third grade and my teachers name was Mrs. Carrington. She had red hair and today I think she had then looked like Carol Burnett. I had gone to school with my thumb wrapped up in white gauge. At the end of the school year she said that she had to keep me back in the same class next year. I remember begging her not to do that because my dad would be very angry at me. I promised her that I would do really well in fourth grade if she would let me pass. She passed me and I had a great fourth grade teacher. Her name was Mrs. Rachford. I had thought she was the most special, nicest, prettiest person in the whole world. Sometimes she would even take me home to her house for lunch. I had asked her to adopt me but she said that she couldn't. I did not get very angry with her because I knew that she was one of the smartest people that I had known at that time and she was nice to me. I did do quite well in her class.

My dad would help us with our homework. One night I remember sitting on a stool next to the table. He was helping me with my math, and I hated math. Anyways he had asked me a question, I had answered it wrong, and his left arm, hitting me in the face with his left hand knocked me onto the floor. I did have a swollen lip and cheeks when we were finally done which probably could have been an hour or more later. From that time on, I had studied and studied and studied. I must have done well in school because that was the only time that I do remember him helping me like that with my school work. I loved reading the SRA books in fourth grade that were available to me in school. The SRA books had come in several different colors. Today I know those colors had meant different stages and levels of reading. There were no books that I can remember in my home, so those books were my adventure. I remember reading and reading and reading. I had finished those books and felt so good about myself that I had done a great job. I know that I had done a great job because Mrs. Rachford had made such a big deal out of it and had made me feel great about myself. Today I give her most of the credit for me being able to read and comprehend what I am reading. I cannot actually find an appropriate word for how I feel about being able to read so well and for also being able to comprehend. I love to read and I have learned how to write different things in a coherent manner.

We had floor metal heaters in the bathroom of the house on Sayre Street. I remember many times that Jo and myself had to kneel on the heater, while the heat was on and the metal had been very hot. We had to kneel on that heater for hours and when they had let us off of them, I could barely walk. I wanted to cry and I did when my dad was not around but when I had heard an adult come near us I had hurried up and wiped my face. I use to have the wettest hands from all of my tears that I had wiped off so that no one could see that I had been crying. If we cried, we would either have to stay on the hot heaters longer or the dad figure would whip our backsides. So there definitely was no crying from either of us that they could see.

When I was a young girl, our parents would hardly buy us anything. No clothes and no shoes. On one of the blocks from my house, there was what I had called a rich girl. Her parents had bought her everything and anything that she had wanted. I had to wear my boy cousin hand me down clothes and his black tie shoes and I had hated all of them. That girl had lovely black, paten leather shoes that I had just loved. So one day I remember telling her that if she did not give them to me I would beat her up. I also told her that if she told anyone that I would beat her up. So now I have these nice black shoes; however, they were too small for me. Now I had a choice, wear the boys' black tie shoes that fit or wear the too small for my feet black pretty girls' shoes. I wore the girls' shoes for a long time even though they killed my feet. I guess this last paragraph proved that what my parents had done to me I had figured that I could also get away with it.

My dad's dad, Grampa Forwell, had baby sat for us for a short while. He had been an alcoholic that I had learned in later years. I remember one day while we were lying on the blanket with him in the back yard, he said, there's gonna be a whole lotta singing here tonight. He used to tell us that when someone was bad and we were going to get our butts whipped. It seems to me that not long before this day, my dad had put some caulking around the windows and someone put their fingers in it. All five of us gathered in the garage for a pow wow and convinced my younger sister Jo to say that she did it, and if she did we would give her a ring. She said that she did it but we all got a really bad whipping with the belt that day. To this day, none of us remember sticking our fingers into that caulking. He, Grampa Forwell, would let all of us kids have his empty beer bottles. We would take them to the corner store and buy all of us candy. Wasn't he the best? All of us kids had to be in bed by 8:00 pm every night of the week but on Saturday night's Grampa Forwell would baby sit us and let us stay up and watch boxing with him. He said that we could stay up until we had seen the headlights pull into the driveway, do not tell anybody that he let us stay up and that we did not make a sound after we got upstairs. Of course we did not make a sound and we definitely did not tell anyone. One day I remember riding in the back seat with Grampa Forwell, the car had stopped, and his belongs and he were put out to the curb and then we drove off. We weren't aloud to make much noise so I had to cry to myself. My dad had thrown his dad to the street because Grampa had a drinking problem. I sure hope that we were good for him and not have caused him any stress.

My dad's mother, Hazel, came to stay with us for awhile. She was a horrible lady. She never smiled nor laughed with us. Today she had reminded me of one of those strict military social workers that you see on the old war movies. She would go around the house with white gloves on and check everything for dirt. She would check over the windows and over the doorways. If she found any dust or dirt, yep, my dad would have to beat us when he got home from work, which was usually after 2 am. So she had found the dirt and we had to clean and clean and clean. Remember, I am in third grade trying to clean a big two-story house with my sisters and a little brother. Actually, if I remember correctly, no one decorated the upstairs, however, she did have us sweep and wash that wood floor. We had a bristle broom to sweep the upstairs wooden floors. Once in awhile a bristle would get stuck in the floor and Hazel would come over and hit me in the head and ask me why I was being so stupid. Once in a while we would be allowed to use a stringy string mop and you guessed it, while washing the floor some of the strings would get caught on the wood and would pull some slivers off the wood. Hit right on the head and being asked why are you being so stupid? I believe that it had been her that would wash our clothes in the old fashion wringer washer. One of us four older children, I believe it was Jan, had gotten their arm stuck in between the roller. She just cried and cried and then we all cried with her, however, even though she was badly hurt they did not take her to the doctors. Her arm was not broken, just badly bruised.

Lucky?

One day there was another lady at our house. I am not sure, but I think I was ten years old. Anyways, she seemed to be very nice, dark long curly hair and she smiled, laughed and talked to us. She would make us a lunch that included a pickle, chocolate bar and a sandwich. I use to love the way she made our lunches. Remember, we never got a lunch to take to school and eat when we were hungry. We only got candy when Grampa had given us his beer bottles. Not long after she was there, I believe perhaps a year, she and my dad had gotten married. And not long after that, a dormer was built onto the backside of the upstairs. Soon after the dormer had been built a room had been built onto the lower back section of the house. This last section that had been built had extended all the way across the back of the house that made a front room for the love birds and a large kitchen for everyone to eat in. The old kitchen had become a dining room which was only used on holidays. In the afternoon and evenings, Shirley would sit in her own living room, while dad had been working, in a spot where she could see whoever was going in and out of the kitchen. She had two children. Nancy, who was very pretty, slept in the front downstairs bedroom and through the years had stuck up for us most of the time. Her son Jack had been a somewhat spoiled child. Actually what Jackie wanted, he got.

The dormer that was built on the back side of the upstairs had two bedrooms that were nicely decorated and the other side of the upstairs was nasty, nothing was done to it. Little Glen had to sleep on one of the nasty sides. Jack had gotten one of the bedrooms and my sister Jo and I had gotten the other. Jo and I would play Barbie dolls for hours in our new room. I don't remember a lot of how things had gone during the early years after Shirley and my dad had gotten married except that in the beginning I had thought she was a special lady. The first time that they had bought me a bra was after Jo and I had gone to the store and stole one. The security had caught us and the male cop constantly talked and checked out our breasts. He was awful. They took us to jail and Shirley and Bob Sr. would not come and get us. They had sent Uncle Tony to get us. He had kept us calm but did let us know that they both were waiting for us and boy oh boy were we in trouble. He was right as always when we got into trouble; he came and bailed us out. That however, was my first and last time in jail.

Uncle Tony was a great dude. He made shoes for a living and had many kids. Before Shirley and Robert Sr. had married we would visit Uncle Tony and Aunt Tilly's house every weekend or most weekends. They had a really large house with many bedrooms, if I remember correctly three floors of rooms. In most of the upstairs room were great hiding spots. You could hide for hours and no one would find you. I just had a horrible thought; maybe they did not want to find me. Their house was the neighbor of the drive-in theatre. The fence that was between them and the theatre was partly knocked down so it was easy to get through it literally. Most of the boards had been broken or torn off so we could fit right through without any problems. When we went over to their house we could go to the movies for free and most times after we were done playing hide-n-seek we went and watched the movies. Today it seems as if Shirley also had done her job of making sure that none of the family had gotten along because after Shirley had came to our house we did not see those cousins again too often. Years later we did have a somewhat of a family reunion but it turned out terrible. I really think that Shirley had told them so many lies and had done so much nasty things to all of us that when we did see many of them again they were rude and seemed to be very uncomfortable to talk to us. Uncle Tony's son Bruce, I remember that I use to call him Brucie, was the boy cousin that I had mentioned earlier where I had to wear his clothes and black tie shoes. Cousin Johnny and Gilbert used to also be great guys before Shirley came into the picture. Cousin Carol was also a cool chick. She had all these brothers and she was the only girl. She did have it rough because she was like the second mom for her brothers helping her mom, Aunt Tilly out. I really liked her a lot while we were growing up. After the family reunion we had talked some however it seemed to be a strain for us to communicate with each other. Again, I feel that Shirley had also put a damper on our cousin/friend relationship.

Anyways, Jo and I had walked into the kitchen with our new bras in our hands shaking like there was no tomorrow. Shirley had been waiting for us in the kitchen. She was sitting in her chair with one leg under the other at the kitchen table like always. She especially would sit like that when she was going to whip our bodies. She would just stare at you, then make statements, then ask questions, make more statements and then up out of her chair and wham. Sometimes she would hide behind the back door and after we would get into the kitchen a few feet she would charge out at us punching us wherever she could. At least when she was in her chair you could see her coming, when she would hide behind the door when you walked in, we surely did not see that one coming. Anyways, I cannot remember which one of us got it first or the worst. She hit us in spots where our clothes would hide the marks that she left on our bodies. She would grab hand fulls of hair on our heads and ripped some hair out causing me to have some bald spots. She would grab at our clothes, ripped some clothes off and tore my blouse open ripping the buttons off. While she would be grabbing and ripping my blouse off she would also grab some of my skin. Some of the skin would be in her fingernails and she would leave scratches on me. When she was done mauling us she would then kick us out of the house but we were not to leave the yard nor let anyone see us cry. After all that mess was over, we had gotten the new bra to keep and was told that we better not ruin it. Shirley basically did hurt our bodies if not everyday then every other day. You would have thought that I would have gotten use to it. I believe that on the days that Shirley and Robert were fighting is when we would get hit the worst. She would take it out on us. A couple of times they would be fighting and she would take us with her to their lake house at Lake Michigan, Little Paw Paw, it was called. A couple of times it was great and other times I wish that I had stayed home with my dad. But then they would make up and he would come up there anyways.

When I was a small child, I had wet the bed every night. It didn't matter if I didn't drink anything past a certain time, which many a night I was so thirsty, especially in the summertime; I still had wet the bed. Up in the attic, there were only two windows, one on each side of the large room which did not allow much air in. There were no dormers or room dividers up there to separate the rooms yet until about a year or so after Shirley had moved into the home. The urine smell upstairs was horrible and sickening especially on those hot summer days. On those hot days, no adult would allow the upstairs area neither to have air-conditioning nor to even have a use of a fan. I never got a new mattress, and boy oh boy did it stink from the urine until I was in the teenager years. I almost think, years later, that I had someone else's bed because of the horrible damage there was to the mattress, but, then maybe not because I sure must have wet my bed a lot. Anyways, every night I had wet the bed. I do not remember ever getting clean sheets or even seen my sheets getting washed. I would have to take the sheets off let them air dry and then put them back on the bed. Shirley would make me sit with the wet sheets on my head, upstairs where it was quite hot and not much fresh air could come through the small side windows. I would have to sit on the wooden floor for hours like that. I did not dare to disobey because if you remember, she had a way of enforcing what she wanted you to do. Other times if I had a friend come over and we were outside playing, Shirley would make me get the wet urine sheets, bring them outside, sit on the ground with the sheets over my head, lying on top of my body with no air holes, in the hot sun, not in the shade, while my friend had watched me. I was so embarrassed that I quietly cried underneath the sheets. I really do not know why I had a mattress on my bed because there was a very large hole in the middle of it that I fell through and was sleeping basically on the piece of wood that was under the mattress. At least I did not have to sleep on the springs, but then if I remember right, there were no springs on my bed.

One time after the adults had gotten married there was a party at the house on Sayre and I drank all of everyone's drink that was left sitting anywhere. I had gotten so drunk that I passed out. I woke up in my bed with a rag in my mouth. By the look on everyone's face, I had gathered that I did not say very nice things. No one has ever told me what I had said either so I guess I will never know.

Nancy, her daughter, was going to school to become a hair stylist. She had long gorgeous hair and fixed it everyday. Since Shirley had ripped a lot of my hair out, I had Nancy cut it really short. After I did, Shirley would call me a *dike, butch or b—-h* and so many more nasty names. Now she could not just grab my long hair she would have to work harder on grabbing it and she did not have too much in her hand after her grabs. After awhile I really believe that Shirley needed some psychiatric treatment.

One day, I had come home from school and Shirley was very angry. She was yelling about something and I didn't know what it was about, however, she had thought I did. She was screaming and yelling at me, ripping my shirt off and pulling my hair out. Then she started punching me in the stomach. She also had long strong thick finger nails that when she grabbed my skin she would take pieces out of me. What the heck, here this nice lady turned into a real psychotic. Almost every day she would do the same thing to me. I had never seen her hit my sisters but I had seen their bruises. It was as if she was afraid to hit us all at once. There were so many times that I had wanted to hit her back and she knew it. That is when I had made a big mistake, because she would hit me harder. She had those long thick solid fingernails that would dig into and claw my skin. I had gone to school when she first started hitting me, and I told my teacher, but again that was a mistake, because now my dad would get his 2 x 4 and bust me with it. I was only eighty pounds in my freshman year of high school. I had been ninety-nine pounds when I had quit high school. Wow, I just remembered what the big problem was that she had whipped me so badly and it follows in the next paragraph.

One day I was taking a bath and the water had become very bloody. I had started yelling and screaming hysterically and everyone came running into the bathroom. Of course the female adults were laughing at me but what the heck, help me. That day I had started my menstrual period and Shirley did explain a little about what that meant. She had discussed how the pad things would be used and had worked. Many of the months that I did have my menstrual period while living at home she did not provide me with napkins and I would get so freaked out what I was going to do. She also had said something that had freaked me out. There should be no reason why blood would be on my underpants. So she had better not find any. I had gotten blood on them and was so afraid to do what with them and I believe that Jo and I had hidden them in the dresser drawers. She had found them. She also had told me that I had better not wet my pants. I must have hid them in the draw also. So now I guess she had a reason, so she thought, for beating the crap out of me.

Every Friday night she would make my dad and her lobster with butter sauce. In their little front room she would try and make a seductive romantic evening for the two of them. Each one of us girls would have to clean up their cooking mess if we were the lucky one to be home on Friday nights. It had seemed to be that almost every dish had been a mess. Just out of the new kitchen was a utility room. The sink actually was used for the washing machines excess water. We use to have to stand on a stool to even reach half way down into the tub. At least once a month if more often, I remember that one of us did not wash the dishes clean so Robert Sr. would empty all of the cabinets and we would have to rewash all the dishes, and God help us if any of them had been broken. We sort of lived in the country where we had septic tanks and not lucky enough to have city water and sewage. We were not allowed to use much water except for washing dishes and/or washing up messes within the house and yard perimeter. It seemed like every couple of days, Shirley would take a nice pretty smelling bath and Nancy would take her bath second, right after Shirley in the same water. Jan, Jo and I would have to say quickly next in order to get bath three, four, and five in the same water. My little brother Glen would always have to be last to take a bath in all of our filth water. I use to feel so badly for him but what could I do? I do remember that everyday Shirley had always smelled fresh as if she had taken a bath earlier that day. I had found it to be interesting that she took a bath in daytime hours but one or two times in the evening. Before she had moved in we had taken a bath several times a week and if we did not then we would get our butts whipped. Today I know that you do not use a lot of oils in the bath because it causes some type of buildup in the septic tank. I also had found out that if the tank had been cleaned every two years, one would not have to worry about how much water would be put into the tank.

Grandma Billy and Grampa Billy were great people. I thought that it was great that both of their names were Billy. He was my birthmother's dad and she was his second wife. He would have a refrigerator on his back porch full of all flavors of soda for us kids to drink. He would get out his game of croquet and set it up for all of us to play. It was great, drink cold soda, laugh and then have to go home and go to our rooms. I just loved going over there but after Shirley married my dad we didn't get to see much of them. Shirley did not like grandma, though. Shirley would be so rude and mean to her and then she died. Grampa died one year later and they would not let us go see either of them at their funerals. They did state, however, that if I had black shoes then I could go to the funeral. I did not know what a funeral was, but it was going somewhere. I did not have any black shoes but I did have some white gym shoes and some brown shoe polish. I remember polishing the white tennis shoes a nice brown color and then later I was doing a whole lot of singing. There were times when Shirley also had made us stay outside a lot and I would hide by a tree that had fallen after being hit by lightening. I had felt as if Grampa Billy was always talking to me before I knew he was gone to heaven. I just had felt peace many times when I was afraid after I had thought about him. Jo and I had built a fort in the prairie across the street from our house. The prairie had really tall grass with a bunch of rocks and tree limbs so not many people would walk through it. The tall grass would lay flat if we walked on it so we would get into the fort by the back way. We would never walk on the grass on the side where anyone in the house could see us so that made our fort camouflaged. Our fort consisted of a big hole in the ground that we covered up with whatever we could find. I think Jan had stayed with us too. We would stay in there a lot when it was cold out and when we didn't want any body to see us.

I remember once I had asked Jo where she was all the time and she said that she had a babysitting job. I had heard some stuff going on but I wasn't quite sure what was going on. Jack (step-brother) liked Jo very much and anything basically Jo wanted Jack had made sure she got. While Jo was dating Jack, Shirley never hit her once. I do remember that Jo had worked at Dunkin Donuts for awhile. One day I had come home from school and they had said that Jo had been sent away. I do remember now that Jo had a babysitting job and the husband was very nice to her. Something happened and Grampa Billy knew about it but nothing really was said that I could figure out what happened. Someone had brought her home and after a few days I had not seen her again for a very very long time.

I know Jan had stayed away from there because I hardly had seen her any more. I do remember at the young age, Jan had to do the ironing and clean the house. Jo and I had to help but it seems that Jan had gotten the worst of the abuse. Shirley used to terrorize Jan really badly and beat her up even worse sometimes than me. It wasn't often I seen Jan get hit but when I did, wow. I remember Jan had gotten a job at a nursing home and I believe that is how I had gotten the idea to work there. She also had a boyfriend and then they had gotten married. I was so glad for her because she got to move out. I think Jan was more excited and relieved than I was.

The way that Shirley had said different things made me very afraid. Shirley always had a way of telling me stuff and/or the way she will say things that scared me. By the last two sentences, I mean that anyone in our life that I had thought was descent; she had made sure that I had become totally afraid of them. She would tell us some horror stories about the birth mom that would make it seem like Shirley was a saint. One Christmas Shirley had told us that Jean had given us a pair of used socks. Then she went on and elaborated how nasty Jean was. I remember Jean had come by one day and I was totally freaked by her presence that I did not get close to her. She seemed to be okay but you just do not know do you. It had been so long since the last time that I had seen her that I forgot what she actually looked like. A couple of hours earlier I had been at the store with some friends and they had stolen some stuff but I didn't and after they came out of the store a guy ran after them and grabbed their arms. He grabbed them and pulled them at him and took the stuff that they had stolen and was yelling something and I was freaking out. He then had told us that he was going to tell our parents. I did not know how he could find out where I had lived unless he followed me. I remember hiding in the back yard when this lady came walking up the driveway. It was Jean, the birth mom. So when Jean had shown up shortly after we had gotten back from the store, I thought she was there to tell on me. I had thought she was the person that was coming to snitch on me.

Fifth thru Eighth Grade

In the fifth grade, at eleven yrs old, I must have been a bad child. I had an old lady teacher who wore those ugly black heeled tie shoes. She had put me under her desk and every time she sat down in her chair she would kick me. Even when I was sitting at my desk she would throw the black eraser at me but she would miss. By sixth grade, I was twelve years old and in the seventh grade, I was thirteen years old. I do not remember much during those years except for Shirley beating me up; ripping my hair out in bunches, cleaning up her messes, and babysitting the two babies. Not long after Shirley had moved into the house on Sayre, new carpeting had been laid and new furniture had been bought for the front of the house front room. It was supposed to be a front room for the children, but the Forwell children, my siblings and I, had no rights in the room. In front of the couch was a two layer coffee table that held a lazy Susan. I do remember that she would buy candy for the lazy Susan candy dish that was sitting in the middle of the front room table. We were not allowed to touch the candy nor were we allowed to sit on the couch. We were allowed to sit on the floor and watch what they watched on TV and only have a piece of candy if she gave it to us. Of course, she gave us a piece after her and her daughter were sitting there eating it in front of me. She did not allow us to watch TV too often but when she did, of course, I thought that was great.

In the eighth grade, I was thirteen to fourteen years old and we had to memorize the constitution of the US if we wanted to move onto the first year of high school. Of course I had that constitution memorized because I was getting out of grade school. The adult figures would not buy my sister Jo or me a bra and that is why we had stolen one each, got caught, sent to jail and Uncle Tony had picked us up. In eighth grade I did have big breasts and was made fun of because of that. I had been and still am very self conscious because of all the rude remarks that the adults would make to me. As far back as I can remember my dad would call me *big boobs*. I just hated that but he would not stop. He always laughed after he would say it.

One of the boys that lived on the next block was called scurvy. I do not remember why except I think that one of the other kids said that their house was filthy. There were enough of us kids total from both blocks where we could play softball, soccer and basketball. All of us kids played with many other kids that had lived on the other blocks. Many of us were about the same ages and had gone basically to all the same schools. I remember that when I had graduated from eighth grade I had been given a fifty cent piece wrapped onto a chain for graduation from the parents. Wasn't I one of the lucky ones? Now I was going to start high school and someone had to bring me there one night to sign up for school. Of course the parent figures would have no part of it. Nancy had done the parent's job like she had done so often during my childhood. I guess I was finally a teenager and had to hear and learn everything pros and cons of becoming one. I am not sure if all of the girls were told what I was told but I do remember some really bad nonsense that they had told me. There was one instance where they had told me that if I had held a boys hand, then I would become pregnant. So, of course I never held a boys hand until I had known better. We were allowed to go about a two block radius from our home. We were allowed to go the distance only as far as we could hear my dad whistle. When he whistled we all only had a few minutes to get home. Of course we did not always hear his whistle. I had figured at a young age that even if I was a really 'good girl' I was still going to get beat up, so why get so stressed over it?

In my freshman year, at lunchtime, I remembered that one of the guys hit me in the head with a carton of milk. I still do not know why, but he was always in trouble.

I was a sophomore in high school and started dating one of the boys on the next block. He had turned sixteen and had a job after school. I could see his driveway when I looked through my bedroom window. We would go out a couple of times a month. I guess we were dating or just going out when he had made me a going steady ring that he had made in shop class. I guess we did kiss some but I never had sex or any really romantic situations with him. I would go and visit his mom and talk with his dad. They were really nice people. In the end of my junior year of high school we were still dating when I had heard he had gotten a girl pregnant. That had depressed me so badly because I actually believed that he and I were going to get married one day. So I had walked around the block and put his homemade ring into his mail box and did not talk to him again for a very long time.

I also had to wear these ugly, dark brown funny shaped glasses that were my dad's. They had broken in the middle of the frame and I had figured out a way to keep them together while they were on my face. I had twisted a rubber band around both lenses where they would pull the middle together. At least I could see a little bit. They finally did buy me my first pair of glasses but I do not remember what grade I was in. I have to figure that the reason why they had bought me glasses was because maybe an authoritive figure told them that maybe they had better. Yes, I know, such a silly girl thinking such a silly reasoning. After putting on my first pair of glasses I was so amazed by what I had seen. Trees were not a bunch of green blur; they had separate leaves that were so neat looking. People had faces that had eyes and a nose and they were no longer a blur. Getting my glasses was one of the best experiences of my whole life. Just think of it, not being able to see anything for years and then one day I could see things so clearly; some of the things I was not sure what they were. I really believe that because of all the carelessness that the adults had done to me as a child has caused me many health concerns today. In 2004, if I remember the date correctly, my eye doctor had told me that I was going blind in my right eye. Isn't that just wonderful? I just say, life goes on and I just have to do my best one minute, one a day at a time.

High School

In the ninth grade—first year of high school—I was fifteen years old. I had started working at the nursing home across the highway from the high school after school because I had lied to them and said that I was sixteen. Shirley had stopped hitting me for awhile and I got a little nervous about why. I guess her son had said that he liked me. I had let him know that he was my stepbrother, and nothing more; however, he did not take no for an answer. He had moved out of his bedroom and rented it to me for pretty cheap. I had thought. Okay, I had thought that was great. On my days off of work Shirley was nice to me because she also had wanted me to stay home from school. At first when she would pull her little stunts you went along with her in hopes that she didn't punch you out that day. I would stay home from school on the days that I did not have to work. My day off consisted of ironing her clothes, cleaning house and babysitting two little kids that lived with us. One of the kids, a little girl named Sherri, had been taken from a college student that had gotten pregnant. She had to get rid of the baby so Shirley and Robert

Sr. had taken Sherri. They had said that Shirley had the baby and no one better say differently. By now I was hoping I was getting smarter. The other baby, a little boy named Jerry, was Nancy's baby. They actually were very cute but horribly spoiled. If little Sherri did not stop crying, I had to take care of her because she bothered Shirley. No, I did not have a choice at the time.

Shirley had charged me rent every week for the room that I had. When I had a day off I had to do all the chores that she didn't like doing; I started working as many days as I could. I never took a day off from the nursing home. Even if I didn't have to work that night, I would go by there to visit. I know that Shirley knew that I didn't have to work that night but did she really care? The babies were older now and she didn't really need a babysitter. I had to give Shirley my whole paycheck every payday. I really do not remember how much I had brought home. No matter how much I had made, Shirley gave me $20.00 from each paycheck. From the $20.00 I had to pay for my own clothes and transportation to and from school and home from work. If I had run short of money that week, I would have to run home from work. All through high school I had owned two skirts, a blue one and a black one. I don't think I had gained any weight through high school; I feel today that it was a great thing because I could not have been able to buy any clothes. I was always a skinny rail with big breasts.

I was fifteen years old and had told the nursing home across the street that I was sixteen. I had gotten a job there right after school from 3:00 pm until 11:00 pm, but sometimes I had to work late. I had gone to school from 7:00 am until 2:45. Shirley had stated that I had better be home by 11:30 after work. In the beginning I would run most of the way home. A bus driver would see me running home and one night when I could afford to take the bus, he had asked me why. I told him and every time from then on if he saw me, even if I had no money, he would stop and give me a ride. I had told Shirley that some weeks I did not have enough money for bus fare, however, she said she didn't care and that I had better be home by 11:30 pm *if I new what was good for me.* I guess I might have been working for about six months and decided that I could no longer run to get home by 11:30 pm, especially if I didn't get off work until after 11:00 pm. Since she had been so abusive to me for so long, at first I was terrified of her, but then I started standing up to her more and more. She did not do a thing to me when I had gotten home. Geeeees, all those months of being freaked out, however, I never really pushed my luck with her.

During my high school years, I had met two great female friends. They were the best friends that anyone could ever want. I am not going to tell their full names, but their first names were Pam and Maria. We use to hang out after school all the way through high school. They both had lived with their parents, which to me, they both seemed to be quite happy. Actually, one of them lived with her dad and one had lived with both her parents and her brother. Anyways, Maria had a driver's license when we were in high school and she would meet us somewhere and then the three of us would go to the parking lot near Evergreen, Ill. In that parking lot was a White Castle, which we called 'whitey one bites'. That parking lot seemed to have been the hang out for most of the teenagers my age and a little older. Sometimes I would get into a shopping cart, hang onto the car and they would drive me around the parking lot. We never got hurt nor did the police ever catch us. I use to walk to Pam's house many times during the week without Shirley knowing it. She would not let me go if she knew, so I would sneak to Pam's house. Remember the long way that I had to walk to grade school? Well, Pam had lived not far from that school and I would walk to her house with no problems. She and I would walk around the blocks having a great time laughing, joking, and talking about whatever. It was really great. She was so funny. I remember that she had curly hair, and in order to keep it straight, she would wrap her hair around cleaned soup cans. That did the trick—her hair use to look really good.

Little Paw Paw is a lake in Coloma, Michigan. Remember, Shirley had taken me and a few of my siblings there. The two adult figures had owned it. One day when I was fishing with my dad on the lake, the fishing line broke after I had slightly pulled it. My dad didn't believe me, so I pulled it with my own hands and it did break, but, I also cut my fingers. He had a cabin off this lake. It smelled horribly like mildew. My dad's mom would show up and use her white gloves; I used to hate it when she came there. I don't recall fishing or swimming very much; however, I do remember cleaning the cabin. We had to do all the hard work inside and outside of the cabin. I remember helping make the brick platform outside the side door. It had to be approximately four feet wide and twenty-four feet long. I remember having to dig the ground with a shovel and if I couldn't use the shovel correctly, I had to use a small shovel on my hands and knees. After the ground was fixed, I would have to carry over the bricks and help lay them correctly. It seemed like every time Shirley and Robert Sr. would fight, us kids (who still lived at home), were forced to go with Shirley to the lake. I think she just did not want to drive by herself. I also remember on occasion she would act like a human being, and actually be quite nice. One time while we were up there she had taken us to an animal farm. I do remember that that was so cool.

In the twelfth grade, I had turned eighteen on January 24th. I quit school not long after my birthday. I never moved before because I was told that if I did, they would call the police. The police would take me to jail and then they would *take care of me when I got home.* I had worked at the nursing home with several nice girls. I had gone out with one of the girls named Linda. She seemed to be a descent, jolly girl. I did not know this at the time, but she had slept with everyone. The old saying, *you are who the company you keep*, must have been quite known by many, except me. She wanted to move from her home and I had wanted to move, so we got an apartment together. We could only afford a one bedroom apartment; however, I had figured that we really didn't need much more. Just a couple of weeks after we got the apartment together, she said some friends were coming over. I didn't know what they gave me to drink, but I didn't know much what was going on. She had gone to the bedroom with a guy and that was that. The other guy stayed in the front room with me. We had talked and joked a lot. Before I had known what was happening, he had me on the floor and was taking my pants off. He raped me. I was fighting with him the whole time but he wouldn't quit. After he was done, he said that he was so sorry because I was bleeding. He thought that because I had lived with Linda that I must be like her. I had felt so much shame that I had believed that it must have been my fault that this had happened to me. I believe the next day I had moved back home. I did smoke some marijuana at the time, but, not really. It was so seldom that I cannot say that I actually smoked it that much. If any of you are reading this and think this would never happen to you, please think again. Of course, times have changed and people act differently, and saying that seems to be old fashion and just does not exist today, unfortunately. All I have to say is that each one of you think about who you are hanging out with and see if others feel that you are just like them. Are you trying to be like them? Or, are you with them because they make you feel needed? Those statements have to go with the question, "Are you you?" You do not need any body; however, you should want to have someone around you without you needing them there.

Friends

After I had moved back home I started working at another nursing home. This time living at home was a little different. I did not let them have all my money this time; however, I believe I paid $20.00 a week, cleaned their house, did ironing, and baby sat on my days off. I had worked double shifts so that I did not have to be at the house very much. I could no longer deal with Linda, so our friendship was no longer. I worked with a very nice (I thought she was nice) lady, Gloria. I had met her son, Don, when he was on leave from the navy. We had dated for awhile, perhaps a year, and that had made her really mad. Gloria had wanted him to date some other girls just to mess around with them. But Don had asked me to marry him. In July of 1971, I had married him. His mom had set up the whole wedding, which I really didn't care. My represented, so-called parents would not lift a finger to help her with the wedding. And of course, they did not attend it either. After we married, we moved to Norfolk, Virginia. My good friend Maria came to stay with us, which I had thought was a great way to start living in an unfamiliar place. We lived together with a total of thirteen people. Most of them were in the military and many of them would be away from the house days, or even weeks at a time. So it was really great to have a friend staying with me. They were all good, kind and funny individuals. We were all friends, and there was no sex between anyone but your own mate. I didn't know this, but my husband, during this time had been sleeping with other females. I do remember that a few of my friends had made several remarks about it, but at the time I had been very gullible, and I did not know what they were talking about. Most of those individuals, however, had taught me that a family origin did not mean that there had to be hitting, screaming or abuse among each other. Each one had taught me something different, and to this day I will never forget any of them. Scotty was a really great individual. He was like a big brother to me. I could go to him and talk about different concerns that I had. He may not have had the answers; however, he listened to me so that I could work through my stuff.

Basically, we were all called "hippies." We all wore bell-bottom jeans, and the females went braless. The landlord allowed us to paint the walls to our tasting as long as we did not ruin the place. So anyone that came into our home had painted something on the walls. I wish I had some pictures of those walls because they were really cool looking and today the pictures would have brought back some many great memories.

We had a lot of people from all over America stop by our house. They would just stay over night or stay for a few days. One evening several of us were sitting on the floor talking and listening to the music. One of the guys that hung around the house a lot was partying with a few of us when he said something to me. I thought that I had heard and knew what he had said, but I did not really believe what I had thought I had just heard.

I had asked him to repeat it again but I still did not believe my ears. So I had moved closer to him, in front of his face and asked him to repeat what he said. He told me that he sure would like to sleep with me. Of course, he used profanity but I had to tell it kindly. I had immediately punched him right in the face. No one has ever asked me that again except for my husband. Everyone around just looked with an amazed look on their faces, then it was quiet for a few minutes, and then we began to sing with the music again.

Anyways, my friend Maria and I would hitchhike back and forth from Illinois to Virginia when Don had been out to sea. One time we hitchhiked to Tennessee. It was raining really hard and the police saw us and chased us because we were not supposed to be hitchhiking on the expressways. They had finally caught us, but, they were really nice. They had brought us somewhere that had dry clothes, some food and a warm bed. So we changed our clothes, ate and went to sleep. In the morning we started hitchhiking back to Illinois. An older couple picked us up, fed us McDondonalds and drove us most of the way home. Those two were really good people. I had thought that Maria and I would be friends forever. After Maria and I had reached Illinois she would go home and take care of what she needed to and I would stay at my in-laws house. I never liked to just sit around, so I had gotten a job at the same nursing home that I had before I had gotten married and where Gloria still worked. So if Don was out to sea for two months, I would work for a little less than two months and Maria and I would be back home to Norfolk, VA before Don had gotten there.

Don and I had gotten an apartment in Oak lawn, Illinois, about a year after he had gotten out of the navy. We had owned a mattress, kitchen table and chairs, a television, some dishes and a chair, and his guitar and amp. We both had gotten a midnight

job at the same factory and then slept in the daytime. On one
Friday night that we did not have to work, we had a party and
invited his cousin Bobby over; I had invited my friend Maria. In
the morning, his mom came by at 6:30 am on Saturday morning.
Any young person that liked to party, and stayed up late knew
that you would sleep late on a Saturday morning. My friend
Maria was there with Don's cousin. Don had opened the door
right after Maria looked out the peep hole and did not quite
get into the sleeping bag before his mom pushed open the door.
Wow, I think it could have been the fourth of July because of all
the sparks that were flying. I will tell you that she had such an
attitude. She was yelling that she had brought over some grocer-
ies, and that we should have been up already and how could we
have let Maria and Bobby stay over. We all basically ignored her
and let her go off and then she finally had left. We had to go over
to her house the next day because Don needed a shave for work
and he did not have a razor yet. He was in the bathroom shaving
with the door shut when his mom started screaming and yelling
at him. I opened the bathroom door and started yelling at her
and Don in the mean time is pushing me out of the front door.
He pushes me down the hallway, through the living room to the
front door where I had grabbed onto something so that he could
not move me. I started to tell her to mind her own business and
started cussing her out while Don had his hand over my mouth.
He didn't want to hurt her feelings, yet, she was allowed to bust
into my house and tell us what to do. I don't think so. She never
did that again. But then we were never friends again. We had
lived in several apartments before we had bought our first home.
In 1974, I had a little boy during the time we had lived in our
last apartment. Don had gotten a job with his dad and I had
worked evenings at the hospital. I believe little Donnie had been
two when we had gotten our first home. At this home we had

our second child in 1976—I had a little girl. Not long after he had found out that I was pregnant with Cari, Don immediately had gotten a vasectomy because he actually never wanted any children, but I did. So, that is basically why I really took the whole load of raising my kids without having his help. And as you will see he was not going to help me for anything. He used to tell lies about me that were horrible. If I had been as hateful as the people that had raised me, I would have sued him. I may not have received any money from him, but I sure would have been ecstatic knowing that others knew he was lying. However, I did not and will not to this day let his lies make me nasty as he may have become.

One day we were on our way to visit his parents and I had seen my sister Jan standing in the middle of the street. She had two little girls with her and was in a big hurry to get to where she was going. We had turned around; however, she was gone. We had moved from the apartment and bought our first house. While we were waiting for the papers to go through, I was very pregnant with my second child. We were staying at some of our friends' house and they were all partying in the living room while I was in bed in the bedroom. Don liked to party a lot and have his friends over, which was okay, but I had a baby sleeping in the other room. I had gone out to the living room where they all were and Don and a young woman were kissing. I let him know that I was there and told myself that when I could get myself together, I was out of there. We had finally moved into the first home when shortly after that I had a baby girl. Two years later we had bought our second home. One day soon after she was born, he had quit his job. During the day I would baby sit two little boys and in the evening I would work at the drug store. Not long after he quit his job, I had found out that Don was selling marijuana while I had worked during the evenings. Later on, I had also found out that he had been sleeping with other women during most of our marriage. During that time, I had worked very hard with myself to keep positive thoughts, and not to let him get me angry. I had to stay strong. I figured that if I had to work to bring in the money, laundry, shopping, the yard work, etc., why the heck did I need three children? (I had included my husband as the third child) We had a big fight and I had kicked him out. Cheryl, a sweet young lady and friend of ours, had been having some problems with the guy she was with and she had stayed at my house for awhile during the time Don was living somewhere else. I had talked to his mom and dad about the situation, but, they did not believe that their precious son could do such horrible things. We stayed apart for about a month or so and then he came back home. I was trying to get the relationship that we once had on some type of positive note because we did have babies. Shirley had been instigating me to leave him. I still had been talking to Shirley because who else did I have in my life? I did not know exactly where and how to reach any of my family members—my sisters, brothers, aunts and uncles. I knew she was right, but I did not want to move in with her because I had figured it would be a nightmare at her residence. One day I had enough of his nastiness, so after I had moved out, he let a lot of people move in. I had an Irish setter that I had raised as a puppy that I had to leave at the house. Don said that he would take care of him, feed him, and let him out to go to the bathroom. One day in the winter I had gone over to the house and had found my little Bilbo Baggins, my beautiful Irish setter, frozen to death, lying on the ground attached to his own urine and poop. I had become so upset and sick to my stomach. How could anyone that had an ounce of feeling do that to a dog? I had to tell the kids that their dog had gotten a girlfriend and ran away from home.

After a short while of moving into this last house, we had met a couple down the street and they seemed to be cool people. Don did get some cocaine now and then that he would sell and have some left over. Sometimes, we, along with our friends, would snort it. I had enjoyed it; however, I believe that because of some of the actions that Don had done made me a little insecure with myself. I do not believe that I had blamed Maria that she was sleeping with Don; however, I did ask her if she was. That is one statement that I have regretted saying for over twenty years. After I had asked her that, she had gone on telling me what a great life I had that I was going to give up. That no she did not sleep with him. Okay, so maybe some of the things she had said and some of her actions had made me a little suspicious about what the heck they were involved with. I finally had enough of his nastiness and I divorced him in 1981. I had thought that Maria was my friend; however, it had turned out to be that she was actually Don's friend and no matter what he said, she had believed and what I had said she must have thought that it had been a lie. I am still hoping to this day that she will accept my apologies and at least talk with me.

This last house was near Don's parents, but better yet, it was near where Jan lived. I had seen her again and found out where she had lived. I had called my dad to ask him if he knew and he and gave me her address. Don and I had drove over to her apartment and by the time we had gotten there, her husband had a large stick in his hand and was going to beat us with it. They would not open the door, nothing. I could not figure out what had happened because I had never done anything to her before in my entire life. I was very sad. We had to leave them alone and perhaps never see her again. Many years later, I had found out that Shirley had told them that I was on my way to her apartment and that I was going to beat her up. Shirley had a way with me and my siblings that made us hate her, yet, we sort of trusted her because we did not know any better. Shirley had been a very sneaky, conniving, and cruel individual that knew how to manipulate situations in order to benefit her.

Nightmare

Would you believe that I had gone to Shirley's new house? I know how stupid I was. I could have stayed at my home with Don and still be freaked out, or go to Shirley's in hopes that it would be better since I had become an adult with two children. She had remarried; I didn't know that Robert Sr. and Shirley had even divorced. Anyway, she let us stay at her house, which was an utter nightmare. I had moved my stuff into her shed in her backyard. I had gone out there to look for something about a month after moving there and the shed had looked like some stuff was gone. I had asked her and she said that no one had taken anything out that she had seen. My children and I had to stay in one room upstairs at her house. Her husband would come home at five o'clock in the evening and I was told that when he got home I had better keep my kids quiet. So after five I would color on the bed with my kids and then go to sleep. She told me that if my kids had done anything wrong. I should hit them for it. I had to get out of there if I was to keep my sanity. I started working at a restaurant and she had babysat for me. I worked there for awhile and seemed to have gotten along real good with one of the girls who had a small son. She asked me to share her apartment, so I did. The sleeping arrangement would consist of the kids in the one bedroom, she in the other bedroom, and I would sleep on the couch. At first it was great. Then she got a boyfriend and he would stay over late and I had to stay up because they would be sitting on the couch, on my bed. She and I started not getting along. One night she went into the kid's room and tried to wake mine up. So I turned the light on and woke up her child and he cried and cried and cried. My two were tired but didn't cry. In a few days I had gotten a trailer. Pam (remember my teenage buddy friend), helped me move into the trailer. I use to hang out with Pam and then we had lost contact. Now I had to come up with some money. I had two young children, no money and was staying in my car. I did have some money in the form of a check at the apartment that I just moved out of but the female would not give it to me. So now what shall I do? Cheryl, a great person, had lent me some money so that I could drive us down to Tennessee. I still owe her the money but no one will give me her address so I can pay her back. Don was not paying child support, how did the courts allow him to get away with that? I had lived many days and months without any money and no food except for some bread and peanut butter. I had told Don that I needed some money, but, he basically told me that it was not his problem. I did remember that Jean, my birth mother, lived in Tennessee, because that is where Jo went to live. No, I didn't forget about her, she just never remembered me. Now, I needed some desperate help for my babies. I did remember she had a friend somewhere around there. I do not remember how I had gotten in touch with her but I did. I talked with Jean and she said that if she came down, I would have to pay for the plane ticket and drive us back down to Tennessee and pay for the gas to get down there. Of course, I said that I would. It was a very long drive because I hardly had any sleep, but we all got there safely.

I had heard a lot of horror stories about Jean from Shirley. So I was somewhat scared of calling her, and going to Tennessee to stay at her house. What else should I have done, stay at Shirley's? After arriving at Jean's house, my kids and I had slept in Jean's den on a pull out bed. She had a three bedroom house. The two front bedrooms were rented out and while I had stayed there part of my rent was to clean their rooms and mow the grass. In the back of the house was the den where I had slept and she watched television and her bedroom was next to the den. She even had a little kitchen off the den. She was always on a tuna diet. She was a real slob. She had called me a slob; however, I had to clean up the whole house and clean up after her. She would let me go out once in a while, but I had to be home by 10 pm. She had let me know that she was not the babysitter. That wasn't very long, but better than nothing. I had seen my sister Jo again, I didn't know it but after talking to her, Jo had run away to Tennessee when she was sixteen. I told her she could have taken me wit her. She had stated that it was an all of a sudden thing and that Shirley had given her an ultimatum and she chose to just get out. Later, I had found out that Shirley had been playing us three girls against one another. Shirley would plant something in one of our dresser draws and make believe that one of us had done it. She had played her games so well with us, that to this day, we all have a distrust issue with one another. I do not have that issue as bad as Jo and Jan do because I guess I had been too smart for Shirley. So she played the game really badly with those two.

Jo had been married for awhile to a real jerk. They had three beautiful children, two girls and one boy. Jo also had baby-sat for many children, everyday and all day long. Her husband had gotten me a job at the bakery. Jo stated that she would baby-sit for me while I had worked and if I had gotten off work early in the morning that I should pick up the kids when they all had gotten up. I was working at the bakery on a swing shift which was hard trying to have a babysitter. I had a babysitter while I was working but not while I was to sleep. One night after I had gotten off of work, I had gone for coffee with another worker. Later that day, Jo's husband had started yelling at me for going out and not picking up my kids. The agreement was that I would pick them up after everyone had woken up and not in the middle of the night. He had checked my time clock card to see what time I had gotten off. Not long after that I had told him to mind his own business or I would tell the boss. I had to find another babysitter, and I did. Finally I had gotten the day shift which had made my life so much easier. I had worked while the kids were at daycare so that I knew they were safe.

Jean was dating this guy who had said that he was single. One day his wife Barbara was over at Jean's and I had met her. I am not sure, but I think Barb and Jean had become friends. Go figure, one becomes friends with the wife of a cheating husband. Barb and I had become pretty good friends so I am very glad that Jean and her were friends first. I could not make myself kiss Jean's backside and had great difficulty keeping my mouth shut. Oh, I was so grateful for her coming and rescuing me and my kids, but did I have to be mistreated by her too? I finally moved out of Jean's house and had gotten my own apartment. Everyone had told me that where I was moving was so unsafe. I did not think so though. We had moved to a duplex and my neighbors were a motorcycle group. I had felt safe there because no one had bothered us. Those young men had become like big brothers to me. They had watched out for my kids when they were outside playing. At 10:00 pm they even turned their music down so that it would not disturb my kids. While living there Barb and her family and I had become closer. I would visit a lot and she would help baby-sit my kids. A short while later, Barb and Wayne, had asked me and my two kids to move into their house, so we did. Barb and her family now became my family. I was happy and then one day she said that I had to move back to Illinois. I told her that I did not want to move back there, she said I had to so I did. Barb had explained that she was selling her home and moving to Michigan. She also stated that I needed to find my family.

Born Again

In 1982 I had moved back to Illinois. The main reason why I had done this is because my friend Barbara said that I needed to do that. I trusted and believed her so I went back to Illinois. First I had seen my brother Bobby and his family. I had not seen Bobby since I was very young and I was so excited at the thought that him and his family would allow me to stay there for awhile. I had stayed there for a little bit but then his wife said that I needed to leave. I could not figure out why, especially because I had been trying to work. But it was only part time. I also had helped clean their house and watch over their kids while there was no adult there but me. I really believe that she had become very envious of Bob and my relationship. Bobby said that he was sorry and I did understand the predicament that he was in. Bobby was a truck driver and was not home very often. When he was home we all would joke and laugh and it seemed as though we were all getting along. He also had a pool table that I loved to play. During the time of staying there I had been working as a waitress and had met a gentleman that I thought was pretty descent. We had gone out a couple of times, and the kids and I would go over to his house and then we would stay over there some nights/days at a time. When Bobby had told me that I had to leave because his wife was giving him a hard time, I had figured that perhaps I should move in with Tim. Tim is not his real name and I am not using his real name because after all that was said and done I had felt so stupid by not trusting what I knew that I knew. So I had moved out of Bobby's house and moved into Tim's house. He had been wonderful to me and my kids so when he had asked me to marry him, I did. We were married about two months when my brother Glen had moved in with us. Glen had been living in a vehicle and I could not have that. Tim had been laid off of work and he and Glen had started getting high while I was at work. I had no clue that they were doing that. Tim started acting really strangely and I had asked my brother about what they were doing and he did say that they had been smoking marijuana pretty much on a daily basis. I did start to notice a real change in Tim that I did not like. One day, I had noticed that Donnie had a bruise on the side of his face and I had asked Donnie what happened and he said that he had fallen. Then I had noticed that Donnie stayed away from the house a lot. Several times Donnie had said that he had fallen and I did become concerned and had questioned Tim. Of course he did not say much about it. I had called Jan and discussed with her that perhaps Donnie had a physical problem and I was going to take him to the doctor really soon. I had gotten a home health care job that had consisted of assisting a man and his wife. She was basically bedridden and I would help him do whatever he needed help with. This was a great job because it paid well and they had allowed me to bring my kids with me and Donnie seemed to be alright then. The older guy just loved them and all of us would talk for hours. I had gotten my sister Jan's telephone number somehow and had kept in touch with her during that time. I had worked for that job for awhile and had made some pretty good money. After work one day, I had gone home and Tim was like a crazy man. He had tried to strangle me with the telephone cord and I had run upstairs to get away from him. My kids had already been up there so I knew that they were safe. I had called Jan during that time and she helped calm me down and had given me several suggestions. Tim started to come up the stairs; however, I had my sewing machine at the top of the stairs ready to throw it down if he came up. Glen had gotten him away from me and said that we all needed to get out of there. The next day in the middle of winter, with a bad snow storm going on, Tim had to go somewhere. We rented a u-haul trailer and Glen, me, and the kids moved the little bit of stuff that I did have into the trailer and we were off. Since I did have some money, I had hurried up to the bank, closed the account and was able to get a studio apartment where the four of us had moved to. Janet, my sister, had helped me get a place/apartment that her mother-in-law had owned. I had gotten a waitress job and my kids went to school during the days where her kids had attended school. I later found out that Tim was still married, so I had gotten an attorney and got a divorce. He had been very angry at me because he had bought some things but the check had bounced. He asked how I could have been so nasty to take all the money. Later I had found out that He had been hitting Donnie but Tim told Donnie if he had told me that he would hit him again and again which made Donnie really afraid of him. When I had found that out I let Tim know that he was lucky that I didn't let some other people know that he had hurt me and my kids so badly. I also had told Donnie and Cari that if anyone had ever hurt them in any way or was not nice to them to immediately tell me. From that experience I had learned that you cannot leave one bad situation and go on to another. I have heard the saying that the grass is not always greener on the other side. I know what that means now, but, I did not know what that had meant then. I had an initial 'gut' feeling that marrying Tim would not be a good situation to move into; however, I felt that I had no other choice at the time. But Tim did seem to me by what I had been seeing and hearing that I might be thinking the wrong thing about him. So I had thought that my gut feeling had been wrong and Tim's actions were what I had figured that I should go by. I had to leave Bobby's house, and what was I going to do? I did not know Jan well enough after all these years to ask her so I moved into Tim's house hoping for the best. Today I have a saying that says, "Trust what you know you know." I did have a choice, however, when I had left Bobby's. I had some money where I could have gotten an apartment. But I did not trust in me enough to feel that I could make it with just the kids and me. Who would baby-sit my kids? How could I support myself if this job would have ended? Something about the Tim situation made me feel uncomfortable, but I did not trust that feeling. Will I listen to me next time?

I had started going to Jan's daughter's church in 1983. On Easter weekend of 1983, I was saved, born again, and had visions. Before I was born-again, I did not know who God was, or what he represented. I also did not know what his stipulations for and in my life were to be. I did know, however, about the Ten Commandments. I felt that what I had been taught at home was not right, and since I did learn about the commandments, I had tried to use them daily to the best of my comprehension. I did not remember all of the commandments, but I did remember do not kill, do not bare false witness towards your neighbor, lie about them, and do not steal. I also had remembered, and still use today is to treat others how you want them to treat you. I have always felt that I have worked diligently on treating people how I would like them to treat me but for some strange reasons most of them have hurt me really badly. Today, I still wonder why that happens so often. Where a good descent individual treats someone else great and they get treated back really badly. I had also remembered the one about God; love only one God; however, I did not know what that meant then. Also, before I was saved, I was always easily distracted and pulled by the outside world. My low self-esteem made me feel ugly and if others wanted me to do something, I usually did it. I always needed to get others involved and invade their time so that I would feel needed. I also would procrastinate about going off alone to think and reflect because I did not want to be alone and I did not have positive things to reflect on. I had been afraid of my own thoughts. I had been afraid of being alone ever since the day that I had found my ex-husband with another female. I needed to be with somebody. So, I guess I basically was an insecure, not-sure-what-to-do-by-myself individual. During those years I had been afraid of so many things and situations; however, I still had to do certain things because I had to take care of my kids. No one else wanted to basically help me. I had to find ways to earn money and to make sure that we had some type of roof over our heads. I was basically all by myself. None of my family was actually available to help me because they had their own lives. So many times I had felt as if I was between a rock and a hard place. If I got a job who would baby-sit my kids? How can I get a place with little money? I had gotten that place of Jan's mother-in-law's apartment because the lady said that she would give me a chance because I was Jan's sister. I do know how some of you feel that have children with no help from others so you do have to make decisions that you may not have made under other circumstances. Because I am so much stronger and independent today I can take care of many of my own situations. I bet there are some of you that are stronger yourself today than yesterday and you try to compare how you took care of things yesterday from how you could have taken care of them today. Sure you could think that and then make yourself feel really guilty about how you handled things in the past. But please do not torture yourself, yesterday is gone and today is here. How you had dealt with situations in the past cannot be taken care of today in the same manner. Why? Because look at your emotions today. Look at how much stronger you are today. Look at how clearer things are today than in your past negative situations. You have to know that many of you have done your best to handle the negative situations of your past.

Today, because I am born-again, I can focus on the future, I perceive time as endless, and I never have enough time to accomplish what I want to do, and I always have time for more of anything. I never procrastinate about really enjoying life today. By the statement that I had just made, I perceive time as endless; when we leave earth we will still live with Jesus. Oh, we may not have these bodies with all this pain, blood, bones, guts and the in-betweens, but we will still be spirits that live and that will be with the Lord. What I believe to be truth may not be what you consider to be truth. Every individual needs to trust in themselves and trust in what you know that you know. I have often told individuals that they should not try and save the world. By that statement I mean that some individuals know that they can make this person do this or that or they feel that if they did this than that person will do that. Stop it! You cannot do it. You cannot make any body do anything. Please stop and think about it. If the Lord has given us freewill, and he does not make us do anything, than what makes a human being think that they are able to make someone do something? They and no one else can make anyone do anything. Oh,

I am sure there are situations, such as in prison where the guards have control of how and where prisoners may walk to or sleep. But they cannot make the prisoners think differently. I am talking about individuals that are living life but perhaps someone else does not like the way that they are living it. If you do not like what they are doing, I suggest that you get your brains and emotions out of their stuff, get back into your own space, and watch and listen carefully to what they are doing and saying and then just plant the seed to them. Just say five to ten words that the Lord and/or the Spirit have given you to tell them. Tell those words, back off, shut up and go on with your own life praying that those words will help them soon. Have any of you been talking to someone and your thoughts went empty? You cannot think of a thing to say? Right. I believe that it is either or both the Lord and your guides telling you to just shut up and watch and listen to what is going on in front of you. How about when you are talking to someone and you start to stutter and you cannot find the words to say? Again, I say, it is either the Lord and/or your guides that are telling you that perhaps there might be something in this conversation that you need to hear or perhaps learn. There are many individuals in this world that only needed a few words of encouragement. I hope that perhaps some words that I have already spoken or will soon speak will touch each one of your hearts and/or spirits to give you some rest and/or direction.

I have met so many descent people, and then many are not so descent. Before I was saved I believe today by looking back I could have probably killed someone. There were some individuals that had taken advantage of my kindness which I am sure many of you have or are going through the same things. Why do people hurt others? Why do so many people try to take advantage of the weak? Why do some people take another person's kindness as a form of weakness? I have so many questions that

I know will basically not be answered. From my different levels of education to this date I can comprehend why some people do what they do to others. Some therapists suggest that many have been abused as a child; that they were molested as a child; that they were hurt as an adult, and I know that the excuses go on and on and on and on. However, I have to agree with most of you, it still does not make it right for one person to hurt or take advantage of another.

I had gone to church with my siblings when I was young. I believe that the adult figures had dropped us off at church and then went on their way. I remember that one day I had been sitting in a pew with some adults. Someone sitting next to me had handed me this gold bowl with money in it. Wow! I thought that was great that someone was giving me some money. So I had taken the gold bowl and just took perhaps a dime out of it. I know it was not a very large amount of money because I was taught that if someone gave you something you better not look greedy or they will not want you to come back to their house. So I had taken my money out and handed the bowl to the person next to me. No one had ever said a word to me that would make me think that I had done something wrong. On the way walking home from church my sisters and I had stopped at the candy store and had gotten us some great treats. I do not think that we told anyone, because, again, I do not remember getting in trouble for doing that. Do you think that was just one of the best gifts that I had ever been given? Before I had been saved I had tried a church here and there and some of those people there were so rude to me. I did not have any nice clothes and they let me know it. Since they were so rude to me and because of those few individuals, I had come up with the conclusion that church going people are hypocrites. In church they would somewhat talk nice to me and then out of church, they were so horrible to me. There are individuals that go to church one day a week and are a Christian. For a few examples, they may drink a lot, they may have a horrible temper and take it out on others, they may be a really bad gambler, or perhaps they cheat and lie to others. Being a born-again Christian does not necessarily mean that you are a church goer; however, I do go to church. It means that you are an individual that knows that there is a higher power that is leading you towards a greater reward at the end of your life. That you can have faith as a mustard seed to know that one day things will be better for you. It is as though you know that you know that you know.

Since I am now a born-again Christian, I know a loving, caring and forgiving God that loves me for who I am. To me, it basically does not matter who on this earth loves me or likes things about me as long as I work diligently everyday doing my best not to hurt or hinder any other individual. It started out when Donnie, my son, and Cari, my daughter, were going to church with Jan's daughters, Janie and Michelle. They were all taking the bus to church. I was very nervous about not seeing my kids, so I had also gone to the church. I sat at the very back of the church on the main floor and just watched everyone. I had figured that I was safe there and no one could really see me and I did not have to talk to no one if I did not want to. Then the pastor had said something and I had found myself up in front with some other people standing there. To this day, I do not know how I had gotten up there. I assume that I had walked up there, but long ago I had learned never to assume. The pastor had continued to talk and out of the corner of my right eye, I had seen people falling down. That had scared me really badly and then I had woken up and was sitting next to an elderly lady holding her arm and I wouldn't let go of her. I must have sat there for more than an hour. I had figured out that conclusion because the church was basically empty. I had continued going to that church, enjoyed it, and started taking classes to find out what had happened to me. At first I had thought that these church people had the devil possess me and I needed to find some answers now. Can you just imagine how much of an angry person that I was from all those years of torture? And then have someone or something knock me out and I didn't even see them coming? It had taken me many months of constantly saying the Lord's Prayer to myself to start feeling comfortable about myself. I had also taken many classes about what the Bible meant. I took classes on spiritual warfare, about angels that are around us, and why and how God had worked with and through each one of us. I had taken many classes that helped me comprehend why I was having so many visions. The great thing that I did learn was that someone loved me. God loved me for who I was even though I had done a lot of not so great things, he still loved me. I even figured out that when I was alone and having a panic attack all I had to do was just keep saying the Lord's Prayer and the name of Jesus. Some days I would say the Lord's Prayer or the name of Jesus non-stop because something had made me so freaked out. After I had said the Lord's Prayer and the name of Jesus, I had felt such a peace come over me so that is one of the reasons why I had kept those two things constantly in my thoughts. If the Lord is for me, than who can be against me? This is a statement that I was constantly confused about. Then one day I said to myself that it means if the Lord dwells within me then no one can keep me away from the Lord. Perhaps that may not be what it means to you but just knowing that Jesus is there for me twenty-four-seven sure does give me some great peace of mind. I was taught that God had given dreams and visions to the elders. Of course, I did learn so much more but those are a few items at this time that had healed my insecurities about me and the fears that I had been facing at the time.

I was working very hard on saving enough money to buy my

own home and as you will soon see that is how I had gotten to Uncle Billy's house in the first place. I am so glad now that I had that experience because he had opened my eyes to individuals like him; I feel that I have become stronger from that experience. As the saying goes you cannot choose who your family is but you sure can choose your friends. I do miss having a family. But then I really do not know what a family means. I have always wanted to be in a family-oriented group that worked together, helped each other, and where you did not have to worry about one of them hurting you. I do not know where I had gotten my views on families. Perhaps it is from being so involved with the church; however, aren't families supposed to love or at least like each other? Aren't they supposed to help each other without expecting payment and/or to be able to say thank you when a loved one helps you or gives you something? Aren't some families supposed to allow other family members to help them out? Why do some family members believe that only they are the ones to help others? Why can't some people see that they are hurting their other loved ones that only want to be loved and needed by them? For many years, I did not know how a mom was supposed to act. In the beginning, I had treated my children like I had been raised until one day when I had heard my daughter screaming and yelling at her baby doll and it caught my attention really hard. From that day on I work diligently on not screaming and yelling. I do not hit them because I did not like to be hit. I have hit my son on several occasions because he would continually provoke me until I could take no more. A great saying that I live by today and have lived by for many years is to do unto others as you would have them do unto you. I have worked on that forever; however, there is no guarantee that others will and would treat you the way that you have treated them. Sometimes I felt as if others had believed that it was a weakness that I had. I treated them how I would want to be treated, but several of them still had treated me badly. Since they are not my problem, and I cannot change them, I constantly keep others in prayer perhaps more than others. Also, today I choose my friends carefully. I do trust my gut instinct and I do allow them and new people that come into my life to do most of the talking. I have learned that when I shut my mouth and allow others to talk, I should know what type of individual this new person actually is like. I know that many of you have some type of vision and when you talk with someone it is as if you are going into their thoughts to see if they are telling you everything. Or, are they lying to you? Okay, so you may or may not find some new information; however, when you were done talking with them and you are now on your way, do you have a different feeling about you? Are you feeling a little strangely? Did you find that perhaps you have some new health issues that you did not have before talking to them? Yes, I could answer those questions for you now, but will I?

I do have my own opinion and feeling about the Trinity. The Father, Son, and the Holy Spirit. One example that I can give is that I am a born-again Christian. I know this because before I was saved, I was a very frightened person. I did not trust nor have faith in anyone nor in anything. I do believe in the Father, Son and the Holy Ghost. These are a few things that I know that the Father, Son and the Holy Spirit have done for me. I believe that by the Grace of God, I am alive today. I believe that Jesus came to earth to take away my sins, heal my body and allow me to have eternal life. I believe that the Holy Spirit abides in me and he is my comforter, guidance and he opens my spirit, soul, body, eyes, ears and mind for spiritual guidance and truth. I also believe that God created the universe and that the world did not evolve from apes. I also believe that man was created by God in his own image and that man has free will. I believe that the Bible is the word of God. That the Bible should be used as guidance for each one of us while living our lives regarding what to do and what not to do in our own lives and towards others. There are two directions that man can go in life. He can follow the word of God or he can do as the world does and commit sin. Sin produces death in the human spirit and this alienates us from God. Since Jesus died for our sins, I have chosen to follow Jesus. What other man in all of time had done so much for us? Because Jesus did this for us, we have salvation. We have eternal life in heaven free from all the sins of the world if we choose to follow. I truly believe that the Father, Son and Holy Spirit are the power of the universe and they have the cure for everything on earth as long as we exercise faith. I really do believe that the Lord wants us to be very successful in everything that we do. I have found that attitudes of all types, whether bad or good attitudes affect the way that we look at different things. I think that how our parents had treated and taught us when we were young affects our lives until we are old, especially if there is no intervention from a higher power. I am a very lucky person because the Father, Lord and Holy Spirit had gotten a hold of me before I had done great damage to myself and to others. Since the Holy Spirit dwells within me, I am very blessed. I am one of those individuals that have been chosen to have visions, learn how to use them, and apply them appropriately to whom they are needed for. Many of you have visions; however, you do not know how to use them. I remember one time when I had first started getting visions, a friend of mine had said that they knew of someone that could help me figure out my visions. That individual wanted to charge me a lot of money to help me and I did not have very much money so I did not get help. Later, I had found out that they did not know what they were talking about. During my time as being a spiritual guidance person at a restaurant, one of the ladies that had gone to that same individual that was supposed to be able to help me came to see me. She had asked me how I had known how to do what I had been doing because she had gone to this other person to learn what I was doing and they had not taught her a thing. I ask all of you to please be careful of whom you are asking help from. I also know that I have enough faith for my body to be healed; however, I have also learned that I have to learn something and be able to apply it before I am healed. How long will it take me to learn and apply it? How long if or when will I be healed?

I also believe that we all have some type of instincts. Those instincts can have many names, such as a gut feeling, intuition, to know what you know, visions, pictures and words in your minds eye, and/or a sort of blackboard in spirit in front of your eyes that have many sentences on it for you to read and even where we may see something from the corner of our eye's. Have you been looking at something and then out of the side of your face, corner of your eye, or your peripheral vision you had seen something move, then you look over to where you had thought you had seen it and there was nothing there? To know what you know, suggests that you believe something is not right and you should trust that feeling.

Right after you see the movement from the corner of your eye, you look back towards where you had seen the movement, but nothing is there. Right? Next time that you see something move out of the corner of your eye, keep looking where you were looking in front of you, while you had just seen that side movement. Just like your visions, you will have to train yourself to see what is in your peripheral vision. I have suggested to others that when you do see something out of the side, train yourself to identify what you are seeing. It can be as similar as the motorcycle or whatever. Try also to envision a spiritual or invisible clock that you can see out of the corner of your eye. Have it set with the same numbers as a human clock. My guides give me a darken shade over the numbers that I am to pay attention to. You have to train yourself to see how to identify your time span. For example, if there is something about to happen in six hours they will show me a six on my clock. If I need to be aware of something, at four on my spiritual clock, it will show a dark on the number four. You will have to train yourself to know what your visions about your spiritual clock are. While you pay attention to your visions, you will be given more than enough information to help.

Many times I have different shades of light colors on the pictures and/or words that I see. Many of my visions will have light or dark over or around the items. When I see black in a vision, I know that is probably one of the worst things that may happen. I tell individuals to be very careful or be quiet and do not do anything that day. When I do see something with a bright light or bright color over or around it, I know that is one of the better days or things that they could possibly have. I always say, check your gut, watch, listen to what is going on and then move slowly.

One night, I had woken up in the middle of the night and had seen several spirits next to my bed. I got my eyes cleared and had seen four spirits sitting at a table next to my bed having tea. I do not believe that they woke me up but something did. Another time when I woke up I had seen a face on top of my face. My first impression was to close my eyes, and then reopen them. A spirit had their face in my face. Later I had learned that spirits do not have any time or space limits as we know them. There have been so many times that I had been shown what an individual's illness had been. I would tell the person, they in turn, if they had believed me, would have their doctor check it out. The doctor took care of it and today they have great health or aspect anyways.

Education

From observing many individuals, taking classes for my Master's degree in Education, and researching many books, I have found that many individuals do not know what to believe in. They allow the professionals, sin, and negative situations direct their lives. They continually try to find a way to fill a void within them. Many try a lot of different negative ways that are continually making the individual very confused. They may think, if there was a God then why did this happen? Some people only believe in the scientific method, others in the Christian method. If one of those methods does not give them an answer, then they usually will use the other method. We human beings are here on earth and have been given free will. Everyone has the free will to do their daily life in a positive manner or even in a negative manner. We all have to decide to use the free will that we were given to do right or wrong.

I have a personal value of life that is diverse from many individuals that I have talked to. Yet it is the same values held with many. I really believe that if I were to listen to everyone's value on how they felt, I would be a prejudice person. As a Family Life Educator, I feel that my value system could work for almost everyone. I believe that everyone is first a human being with feelings. Every individual is important and so are their beliefs. I do not get into any discussions that are leading to one person's beliefs or values. I love to listen to someone that is discussing their values as long as they do not try to make them mine. I know that the Lord had opened the doors so that I was able to get my degree in the field because of my value system. I have the desire to guide any individual that needs help. My value system means that I have faith and I believe in a higher power that assists and guides me in my daily walks of life.

When my daughter was twenty-one years of age she did not like to be told anything. I believe that one reason was because her self-esteem was very low and it seemed like she always liked to do things the hard way. Cari and I continue to have a good relationship but we have butted our heads together a lot. Since I have many visions I have told her what I have seen to guide her. There are many times that it seems she does not believe me. I asked her one day, "If I am telling what exactly you need to take care of why are you not listening?"

She says, "Well how do I know who is telling me, you or the Lord/guides?"

I laughed and said, "If it sounds good, feels right and it helps you make the right choice what does it matter who is giving you the information or guidance."

So, I feel that she is paying more attention today to her own feelings than other individuals that may steer her in the wrong direction.

During my time of studying the bible, I had learned about spiritual warfare. Spiritual warfare, I believe, is where each one of us is not fighting the human being in front of us. Spiritual warfare is where each individual is fighting the next person's hang-ups. Those individuals perhaps do not like themselves, so they take it out on someone else. Some of them have guilt problems of past situations, so the enemy makes them become nasty to others. Spiritual warfare is of a spirit nature that is basically the devil, enemy, and/or negative any thing that is going on between human beings. The enemy does not want any of us to be happy, it wants us all to be miserable and hurt anyone around us. The Lord has given us the Holy Spirit to dwell inside of us to guide us, strengthen, teach, show and give us the understanding of situations before us and of the correct way of doing things. There is a constant spiritual warfare going on inside everyone and everyone needs to be aware of it. Each of you read Ephesians in the bible; there you will find what I am talking about. I have learned that when I get so annoyed with someone it is not because they have actually done anything to me, it is because I have felt something in my spirit from and about them that has made me become annoyed. When I become annoyed, I first go to prayer (not get on my knees and pray), but I might say, "Lord give me the knowledge, wisdom, understanding, guidance, and strength to know how to deal with this situation."

I really believe that the truth is in the eyes of the beholder. Whose truth is the real truth? My truth is what I know that is within my spirit and the facts that I have on the issues. At my age, I have been through things that I would not wish on anyone. At a very young age I was beaten, raped, and almost starved to death. I did go to my teachers at the time the mishaps in my life were going on and they did look into it. The authorities did nothing about the issues that I brought to them because I was a young child. They did not wish to believe what I was suggesting. They had believed the adults in my home. My dad let me know that I had better not do that again if *I knew what was good for me.*

So, I did do my best to survive in his home. It was a real shame that his second wife was meaner than he was. I had told my dad what she had been doing to us kids. Of course she had denied it. What was I thinking? While he was at work, I had paid a terrible penalty for telling him. She had lied to him and he believed her. So, actually what is the truth? If a person can see and hear what is going on, then why don't they believe what they see and hear? I believe that it is because there are many definitions of what truth is and the truths are actually all put together and each individual believes only what they want to. It is almost like selective listening/hearing.

Jean has a brother named Billy and I call him Uncle Billy. I had thought for many years that he was the greatest. He had always made me laugh as a kid and I just loved him to death. I was saving up some money and my uncle Billy had said that I and my two kids could stay with him and his family for a few months until I had gotten a place. I had thought it would be a few months. I paid him rent and bought my own food. He had allowed the three of us to stay in a bedroom. Not long after we were there, on an early Saturday morning, he told me that he wanted me out of his house right away. Of course, I was very upset and asked why, but he wouldn't say. I told him I had just given you all my money, are you going to give me it back? He did not give me any money back nor did he help me move. During the time I had been staying at his house, I was looking for my own home and I was also going to one of the churches in town. I had talked to one of the ladies that went to that church and told her of my predicament and she let my kids and I stay at her home in one bedroom for awhile. I had cleaned her home and whatever I could do to help pay my way. She wouldn't take any money from me. I had asked my ex-husband during this time to help me, but again, he said that it was not his responsibility and the courts said that he did not have to. I had found out later that he had paid an attorney to get the child support dropped and get the case closed so that he did not have to pay child support. I had also gone to Chicago, Illinois to the child support court and found out that the case had again been closed. The lady at the counter had stated that she would get the case reopened; however, I have not heard a word from the Illinois courts since that day.

At this church I had many visions and was allowed to tell the others there about them. At first, I had been very leary about telling anyone, but it seemed to me that others were also telling of their visions and I had felt right at home. The church people did not make me feel like I was a freak. I had found long ago, but I do not comprehend, why those individuals that have visions will not let it be known; however, they will virtually crucify others that have them. There was a black piano at the church and one of my visions that I had seen was a spirit of a lady lying on top of it. I had told that to one of the ladies, and she started to cry and knew exactly what I meant; but, I do not remember what she had said that it meant. I actually wanted to stay there forever because those people were great to me; however, I did not have enough money to get my own place at this time.

I was not there very long when I had, in 1984, moved to Michigan. I had stayed with Barb and Wayne in a bedroom with our clothes hung on a rack. My two kids and I had slept on the floor under the rack of clothes. The floor had great fluffy carpeting and we had a lot of blankets and our sleeping bags as beds. I tell you what, that was so much better than sleeping in my car. Years later, I had told Jan about what Uncle Billy had done to me and my kids, but I do not think that she believes me because she is much friendlier with them than she is with me.

While I was in Michigan, I had gone to a school to become a medical assistant. Barbara and Wayne had watched my children while I went to school. At the time I was on Medicaid and was paying them rent. Her mom lived there at the time and was sick. Her name was Meme and she had a bed in the front room. She was getting on Barb's nerves very badly, so I had helped take care of her. Meme thought that I was very mean because I had made her stay in bed at night instead of waking everyone up. Barb and Wayne basically treated my kids as their own. While I was in school, they took my kids to the beach for a couple of days and treated my kids very good. I had thought that, until one day, her husband had molested my daughter. I did not know this until we had gotten our own place. I was so upset that I had trusted them with my kids. I was devastated. I was going to kill him; however, he had moved from their house and no one would tell me where he was. When I finally had found out where he was, he had died. I was still friends with Barb for a while after that situation; however, another situation had come up and that was the last straw to me.

My son Donnie was involved with the boy scouts. The troop leader and his wife had become our friends. I would help when the troop had an outing to do. For instance, one Saturday, I was the cook all day making some really great pancakes. I also helped with other things and events. The kids and I would go over to their home and stay awhile. I had gotten to know all of their family quite well. I was so glad that I had because a good friend of theirs knew of a three bedroom apartment that had just become available and they all had told the landlord that I could be trusted. I have tried for many years trying to get me and my kids our own apartment, but it seemed that no one wants to rent to a single mom with kids. I had finally gotten my own three bedroom apartment and loved it. I had a bedroom for each child and one for me. I had worked at a couple of doctors offices. In one doctors office I had worked sixty hours a week and got paid for forty hours. During the time of working there, I did acquire more medical experience which I definitely needed. After a few months, I had left and got a job in an eye doctors' office at the front desk. Donnie and Cari had gone to an elementary school not far from the apartment and Barbara lived a couple of blocks away and would stop in on the kids unannounced. I feel that that helped keep them in line and out of a lot of trouble. I worked days from 9:00 am to 5:30 pm, but I did not make enough money to pay the rent. So the manager allowed me to wash the doctors' gowns that were used during eye surgery. The manager also allowed me to water the garden and the grass at the office. I still needed some more money, so Donnie, Cari and I had cleaned the office every night after I had gone home, and made dinner; we ate and went back to the office. It was very tiresome, but I had told my kids that I don't want us having to live with anyone ever again. I had worked there for two years and had found a job that paid more. However, the new job was horrible. I had to work a lot of over time. I really believe that the stress from the doctors and other individuals I worked around that I had worked with and for had caused my health to depreciate. One day, I had asked one of the MA's to give me an EKG and she did. The results had stated that the stress was causing me health problems and I should not be working. The doctors believed in having a lot of medical tests done on their patients. The people that had worked in the back were horrible individuals. I had felt that I was in a competition to see who could do certain jobs that others did not want to do. I did not care what job I was told to do; however; I would have liked it better if those individuals would have been less nasty to me and others and had answered some questions that I had asked them. I was not there long, less than a year, and had gotten fired. Of course, I was upset, and what was I going to do now? I sat in my car down the street not far from my home and cried and cried until there were no more tears. I had been getting a lot of chest pains and other aliments. I had gone to a doctor and she had stated that my heart needed some repair, that I had mitro-valve-prolapse and that I could no longer do hard jobs. I had to go on Medicaid and food stamps, which actually were a Godsend because I had no job and I did not want to loose my apartment. At first I had felt ashamed that I, at my age, had to be on Medicaid. I had done what the doctor suggested to do to improve my health. I was to work diligently and not allow others to get me upset and I was to work to keep stress in my life down to a minimum. Sure that was hard, but I had worked diligently every day trying not to let others garbage become my problem.

While I had worked at the eye doctors' office, I had met a lot of great ladies. One of the ladies, Marie, was a good friend of mine. She and I had been working back and forth with our visions. I would try to guess what she was thinking about and visa-versa. We had gotten pretty good at it. My visions had gotten so good that she had recommended to me that I get a job at a restaurant being a psychic. I had thought that the word *psychic* meant a horrible devil possessed individual. Believe me, I did do my research on that topic. I had thought about it for a long while and agreed to try it. It was wonderful. I would sit at a table while individuals would write their names on a list. I would call them and then I would talk to them. One lady stood up and started yelling at me and had asked me why I had called her mom and had gotten all of her personal information. I had explained to her that she wrote her first name on a list with other names. I had never seen her at the table. The information that I had gotten was from the Lord and my guides. I tell you what; she scared me when she started yelling at me. Another lady had come to my table where I was. It was the day before that she had seen a therapist and had told him about her visions and he told her that she was crazy. She had stated that she was crying and very upset and was on her way to killing herself. Then, my name had come to her mind and was going to give me one chance. Of course, I did not know any of that. We had talked, I had explained about me, what I had seen for her, she had felt better and so had I. As far as I know, she is doing quite well today. So I had worked there for a long time until the lady in charge wanted someone that did not have visions tell people things, to be deceitful to others. I have had individuals in my life that were fakes, they lied so much that they thought it was truth and abuse me so bad that I was not going to allow some fake use me as their way to talk to my clients. Some of my clients that had written down their name on my list were told to go to another person. They tried them and then came back to me, told me what had happen. It upset me much and I quit that place. I really did not make much money and that was not the reason to talk to those people. The reason why I wanted to talk to those individuals was so that I could plant the seed and perhaps give one of them incite that they are worth being alive and around; however, the experience that I had acquired was priceless and my reputation was at stake. I had then gone to another restaurant on Greenfield road in Dearborn, Michigan. I had first talked to the owner and read for him, he agreed that I was not a fake and I had gotten the job. I also started doing reading in my home. Even though I basically did the reading for free, now I did have enough money to stay in my own apartment and not have to get a job that I could not do. My rent was $280.00 a month. I had written down the amount of my rent to let others know that with God's help all of us can make it and you just have to have faith as a mustard seed. Around this time I had met a gentleman named Ted, in 1986.

Ted

Ted and I were going to the same church at the same time called Fairlane Assembly, which I had thought was a great place. He and I had met at this church during a class that we both were taking and we also were going to a Friday night singles meeting. At the church, single people would get together to talk, sing, pray and take classes together. I had also seen Ted in the church parking lot and did not give him a second look until one day he had locked his keys in his van. He had asked me for some help and I helped him. That day we did start becoming more like friends.

Ted and I had dated for four years. I did not want to get married and I did not want to leave my own apartment. Before I had agreed to marry him, I prayed without ceasing for weeks to find the correct answer on what to do next with my life. In 1990, June 2, I had married my second husband, Ted Hagan, at our church. Before we were married, he would sometimes give me some money to help pay my rent even though I did not want him to do that. I truly believe that today, 2006, we do communicate pretty well together. I do know that I still have some insecurities from my past, but everyday I work on them. I believe that I am an organized person, I do not like to leave thing until the last moment. I am not quick to show anger and that may be why some individuals think that they can take advantage of me. Ted did not have the sad childhood as I had so he does not really comprehend what I am talking about at times.

Before Ted and I had married, he and I had visited his children. He had two boys and one girl. Kim, his daughter, and I would meet for coffee at a restaurant near my apartment. I had believed that Kim and I were friends. Ted's second son, Jeff, had his own place and visited a lot and Kim was living with Ted. Jeff and my son Donnie had stood up in our wedding. It seemed that not long after we had gotten married, his children became very rude to me. I just couldn't believe it; I hardly knew these people and they were so rude. I had done my best to keep positive and not let their nastiness bother me. I really believe that Ted had a lot of insecurities and he would talk about them to his children. It was not that I had done anything wrong to Ted; it was his beliefs of what he had thought was happening. Basically, to my face he would tell me jokes and try to make me laugh. I had realized that Ted had a dry sense of humor, and he would be joking with someone and they would take him seriously. I had told him many times, that I am not his ex-wife and I was not there during your troubled marriage. I was especially not involved with Ted until after he had been divorced. We had dated for four years because of his different attitudes that he had gone through. I remember asking him several times during our dating days why he treat me like garbage, then treat me so nicely. My God did not want me to be involved with someone that would hurt me. His attitude did change a lot while we were dating; however, I really feel to this day that he had been saying negative things about me to his kids. One time he had told me that he had walked to work, which was a great distance from where he had lived and I had become so angry about that and I believe that he had only told his kids the part where I had become angry. I do not believe that he had told them that he had given his money to certain people, and not to me, and then he did not have any money to pay his van insurance so he walked to work. There were many days that he was depressed and I would go to his apartment and just talk or pray with him. I had prayed and prayed everyday in my interests and concerns regarding Ted. One day while I was praying I had heard these words. "You can marry Ted, it will be okay." So, I did and everyday I still pray and know that it will be okay.

We had also visited his son, Jack, and his wife, Kathleen's home. They had a baby boy and I had started babysitting him free of charge. I had thought this is how families treat and help one another. I had baby-sat for sometime and my only requirement was that when Kathleen would get her schedule that she would let me know. Well, she never gave me her schedule. She would tell me a few days ahead of time and that would give me no time to schedule things for myself. They also had a baby girl, Chelsea that I baby-sat. One day, I was to baby-sit and Kathleen never showed up. She never called me either and I had become very upset. I had asked Ted to check it out and he said that she got another baby sitter. Why? No one told me why she had gotten another baby sitter. These people were rude. Sometimes I would go to Kathleen's and Jack's home to pick up Chelsea, and Kathleen would tell me that she knows how Ted and I would be fighting. I asked her what we were fighting about. I did not know that we were fighting, and she would tell me to go ask my husband. I really had found it quite difficult to put up with his children's neurosis. One of the kids had cussed me out and said such nasty things to me that I had finally told Ted that if he didn't finally stick up for me and stand by my side, I would handle the situation. I told him that no one again would swear or talk disrespectfully to me and that our marriage was over. I had come too far to allow individuals that I had thought were great individuals treat me with such contempt.

One day, a sister of Ted's had told me that I had better get used to the fact that Ted's ex-wife is the sister-in-law, and I will never be. I had told them that they were full of it and that they better get used to the idea that I am the only sister-in-law that they are going to ever have again. His ex wife had hurt him, and I cannot believe that his family are friends with her. One sister even told me that Gramma, Ted's mom, did not want me in her house. I had become so devastated; my heart felt like it had broken. I would have done anything for her and she knew that. She had always made me feel as if I was one of her own and I had felt the same way towards her. Gramma never had said that to anyone. Instead she would call me up and ask me why I was staying away? How come I was not visiting her? When was I coming over? Ted and I started visiting her again and did not listen to what anyone, but Gramma had told us. I am thinking at this moment, have I made another bad choice? Am I really that stupid?

My brother Bob had gotten hurt in the middle of the 1980's. He had owned a three-wheel bike, and one day while he was riding it, without a helmet on, he crashed in a field near his home. He hit a deep hole and he had flung up into the air and his head had landed on a large rock. He had become a totally different person after that accident. He did have a girlfriend and she worked diligently keeping him stable in all his aspects of life. I do not know how but Bobby had gone to South Carolina where his dad lived. Robert Sr. had a nasty trailer that he had rented to Bobby. I had heard that Robert Sr. had tried to take all of Bobby's money, but Bobby had gotten his head together and wouldn't give it to him. Since he wouldn't give Robert Sr. all his money, he needed somewhere to live. So we let him move to our house. He stayed with us for about two years in our basement. We had set it up where he slept on a pull-out bed couch, because he did not want a bed, which he could have been much more comfortable. We had found him a mobile home in a trailer park not far from us. It had taken a lot of convincing to get him to agree to move there by himself. He was so afraid to be there by himself; however, after he had moved there he loved it. Ted had retired in 1996, so he was able to spend a lot of time with Bob while I was finishing my schooling. Ted would tell me of all the silly things he and Bobby would do and the both of us would just laugh and laugh. Ted and I had taken care of him and then we had gotten some nurses to help him. During that time, I had worked very hard and had gotten my Bachelor of Arts, so I did not spend as much time with Bobby as I had wanted to. Bobby was so funny. Every time he had done something wrong, Ted would know about it and Bob would start talking to me and snitch on himself. One day, right after church, Ted and I had gone to a friend's home for a cook out. After we had gotten home, I had received a telephone call that everyone was at the ER with Bobby. When I had gotten there, Bobby was still in the ER. Shortly after that they had taken him up to his room. I was sitting in the waiting room down from Bobby's room with Ted when I had seen Bobby come from around the corner from his room wearing a white gown. Bobby had passed away and I had seen him on his way to see the Lord. He walked by me and he was smiling so big and he was not limping. I smiled and cried at the same time. As I had watched him go by, all of a sudden, I had heard him call my name, which had startled me. Ted and I got up and went to his room and he was on life support. Bobby had passed away May 29, 1997. He was buried in Streator, Illinois, on June 2, 1997.

Ted's mom, Gramma Hagan, was a real sweet heart. She had leukemia for a long time, but no one really ever knew it. She had a boyfriend named Ken. I really know that he adored her. It seemed that whatever she needed he could do for her. They would travel and go to a lot of church functions. I did not get to know her long, only several years, but I am very blessed that I had gotten to know her at all. Ted and his sisters and I had thrown her an eightieth birthday party. Everyone came and had a great time. Gramma Hagan especially had a great birthday. She had seemed to be very happy.

The night before she had passed, Ted and I had stayed at her house and assisted her with whatever she needed. She had been hurting really badly that night and had asked us to take her to the hospital. Before we had taken her, I had a vision that her apartment was empty. I was assuming that she was not coming back home. I was the lucky one that was allowed to sit with her at her bedside to help her with what she needed. She seemed to be doing okay, so Ted and I had gone home to get some sleep. We had gotten a call several hours later that she was very sick. Actually she had passed away while we were at home sleeping in 1998. I was so upset that I had passed out. I guess that is the way the human body dealt with uncomfortable situations. There is one thing I do not understand. I thought of the saying, "Do unto others as you want them to do unto you." I thought I had been doing that most of my life, and many of the individuals, family, and friends of Ted were just horrible to me. For eight years Ted and I had lived in that house and I had put up with Ted's families abhorrent behavior. Ted and I had discussed that it was time to move on. We both loved to travel, and during those eight years, we would try to travel at least once a year. The last two years,

1997 and 1998, were the hardest times in my life. The brother that I had thought I would never see again had been in my life for a short time, then he died, and that was better than no time. And a great lady, that I had the honor to have as a mother-in-law, my gramma, and a true friend, died. She was always fair to me and anyone else. I had felt that it was a great honor that she had wanted Ted and me to stay with her at the hospital. She had personally requested that I be the one to help her with anything that she needed during her stay at the hospital. I had fought all night to get her into a comfortable bed as soon as possible. Just before we had left, she had gotten a soft bed.

For many years, Ted and I would drive to Illinois, because he had been retired and I was finishing with my school. We would visit my sister Jan, her husband Rick, and their three children. Jan had told us that there was a house for sale in Streator, Illinois, where she had lived. Just before we had sold our home, Ted and I had decided to go there and buy it. So after we had sold our house, we packed up all our belongings and loaded three U-hauls. Cari, her son, Willy, Ted and I were moving to Illinois, and Donnie, my son, had only helped us by driving one of the U-hauls. During our visit, we had put our things in a storage unit until we had purchased the home. We had talked with the owner of the house several times, but things did not seem right to me. We had put a deposit down but we couldn't get the owner to get his part of the deal together. After have a few days with constantly being with this guy, we had found out that what he was selling was not his to sell. Of course, we had to get an attorney and everything had gotten straightened out. Now what shall we do? We parked our trailer in front of Jan's house. Cari and William had stayed in a bedroom at Jan's, while Ted and I had stayed in the camper. We were constantly looking for another home, but somehow things never worked out. Cari was so upset staying there and would say that her Aunt Jan was being mean to her. One day, I was trying to talk to Jan about what was wrong and she freaked out and called her husband to come home. He started yelling and cussing me out, and he started talking badly about Cari. That was enough, I was done. I told Ted and Cari that we were leaving.

We went to the trailer and stayed there until I could figure out what to do. Well it was horrible. Cari rented a u-haul and got all of her stuff moved into it. Cari and Willy had gone back to Michigan. Ted and I had left most of our stuff in the unit since we did not buy the house. Jan and Rick would not help us with anything; they sat on their front porch and just watched us. I did not talk with them again for a couple of years. Since we did not own a home, Ted and I started fulltime camping in the fall of 1998. Donnie had stayed in Detroit at a friend's home and Cari and Willy had stayed at an apartment near a friend of hers.

Ted and I had gone to a campground in Tennessee during the winter for a few weeks, and it was horrible. There had been an ice storm and the ground was so slippery, so as soon as the ground had melted, we had gotten out of that campground. It was actually our first time not knowing what Cari and Willy were doing and it was very hard on me. We had talked to her every week but I knew she was not telling me everything. That winter, we went back to Michigan and stayed with Ted's sister Pansy and her husband Al's home in Roscommon, Michigan. It had snowed so hard that year; the snow was almost up to my mid-section. We had stayed there for a couple of weeks when Cari had called us and said that she needed our help. So we left there and rented a camp site not far from her apartment. The roof had been leaking at her apartment. Things were a mess. Both of them were okay. Cari and Willy moved out of the apartment, and moved in with Ted and I into the trailer and we all got a campsite west of Ypsilanti, and east of Jackson, Michigan.

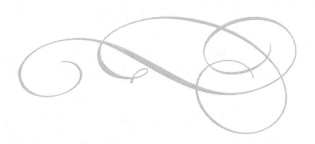

Illness

In July of 1999, Ted and I had bought a house in Ottawa Lake, Michigan. We had moved Cari and Willy upstairs. Donnie still had been living with his friend in Detroit but eventually had moved in with us. I was glad that Ted had been retired because of the way he loved his lawn mower. Every week he would be out there cutting our acre lot and loving every minute of it. I would do all the gardening, plant all the flowers and keep the pond clean and working. It seemed to be a great time in our lives. I had worked as a substitute teacher for about a year or so. In the fall of 2001, I had a mild stroke on the same day that Ted had his second cataract taken out and we were driving the pick-up truck on our way home. I was driving the truck and my left side of my body became all strange. I had just gotten Ted home, and Cari went to get Ted's medicine from the store. I do not know how I had done it; however, I was told that I took care of Ted shortly after having a mild stroke until he was alright. I do not remember much after that; however, I do have some friends around me that were by my side each step of the way. At that time I was in bed for six months and was disabled for five years. I am still counting, but I was told that at first I could get up and sit in the living room chair and then I just stayed in the bed. Ted and Cari had taken care of me. Sometimes they would forget about me and didn't feed me, but I was okay because I wasn't hungry. I had to go to many doctors and had many tests done. Several doctors had told me that they didn't know what was wrong with me. Just because the doctors say they do not know what is wrong with you, does not mean that your aches and pains are not real. Yes, I do know that there are hypochondriacs and attention seekers; however, I am not one of them. Hang in there and you will get some needed help. I also had acid reflux, so I had to get a bed similar to a hospital bed because I no longer could lie flat; it had gotten too hard for Ted to keep adjusting my position. The pain that I had gotten in my chest and back was so bad that I had thought that I was having a heart attack. Ted, on several occasions, had to take me to the ER because I could not deal with the pain. The pain had felt as if a knife was being stabbed through my left breast and through the middle of my chest and out through the middle of my back. I had gone on a very strict diet that my doctor had put me on that forbid me to eat spicy and greasy foods; it was basically a dull, bland, no flavor diet. My chest pains were so bad that I could not even wear a bra. If I had worn a bra for more than an hour, I would get such horrible chest pains.

I had so much pain throughout my body that I did not want to lie down in a soft bed or sit in a soft chair because it would hurt to badly. The pain on the left side of my body felt as if someone was stabbing knives in my shoulder, in my muscle, in my elbow, in my wrist and in my hand. I had to have Ted and/or Cari set up and cut my food because it was too hard to use my hands. I also had a hard time moving my head towards the right. I could move it to look to the right for a few minutes but then the pain would be so great that I had to get my head turned back to the left. The pain that I have gets so bad that I cannot sit nor lie comfortably even in my bed. The pain had also gone through my lower back, down my left hip, leg and through my foot to my toes. Since I could not lie on our soft bed, Ted had gotten me a really soft, special mattress hospital-like bed. My soft bed is so much better on warm days; however, the cold days still cause me great amounts of pain. I had gone to several other doctors which several of them had told me that there was nothing that they could do for me. I have several illnesses and they told me to 'stay warm' and take my medications and get ready to die. That was not the news that I was hoping for. I actually was hoping that someone could help make me well. My body had lighted up like a Christmas tree during the time I had been getting an MRI of my whole body. The doctors were amazed and many had discussed it, but no one could figure out why my body lit up. I also have fibromyalgia, which is the nerve ending of the skin. Every time someone touched me, they would cause me horrific pain. One day in the ladies bathroom at some restaurant, a lady was discussing with me about fibromyalgia. I had told her that I had it and she said that her daughter-in-law had it. She also had stated that the pain could not have been that bad and she had thought that her daughter-in-law had been faking. I certainly was glad that I could straighten her out. A severe case of fibro-myalgia is very painful. When Ted would touch my arm, at first I had thought he was being mean to me. After much investiga-tion, I had found out that my nerve endings were inflamed and he was not being rough with me. I also had to and have to still wear clothing that is really soft on my skin. If the material has any type of roughness I get aggravated because my skin burns; it itches and I get a lot of tender spots by the touch. I also wear very loose clothing. Since I have improved, I can wear a little bit more fitting clothes. The arthritis and rheumatoid arthritis is in most of my body. But as most people with it, you take your medicine and hope it works really fast and for a long time. The osteoporosis that I have makes it very difficult to sit, lay and walk. Heat seems to make it feel better, but the cold makes me sort of feel like you could hurt someone. I had also been taking the medicine called prednisone. This medicine seemed to me like a life saver. However, you could only take it for twelve to fourteen days and then you had to wean yourself off of it. During the time that I had been taking that medicine, my body was feeling really good. I thought it was a miracle drug. Sometimes, when I knew that I was going to make a long trip I would save my medicine and take it then. One problem, however, with taking that type of medicine, is my body swells. At this time, I do not remember what my weight was, but I do know that eventually I was 140 pounds and had gained weight. I was at 200 plus and I am 5 foot 2 inches.

The doctors will not discuss the mass in my head until I have a brain biopsy done. I let them know nicely that they could cut open my brain and do research when I am dead and will not know any difference. The pain that I have in my head is so bad that most days my medicine does not help it go away. For a couple of years, I believe it was 2002 and 2003, I stayed in bed for six months; I had a problem talking and remembering things, I could not use my left arm, and I could not walk very far. I played different games like scrabble on the play station that Ted had gotten me to keep my brain going. I believe that really has helped me a lot. Today, 2006, I am in a wheelchair. You bet I am excited. I do sit up longer than before, but I have to play games with my life. If I sit up all day, the next two or three days I have to stay in bed. One doctor told me to choose my activities wisely. At first I did not know what he meant, but slowly I did figure it out. I do not clean house very well any more. When I do the dishes, it takes me all day, but I do eventually get them done. Do you ever wonder sometimes why you get or have what you have?

Most of the stuff that I have gone through others have gone through too. I worked and prayed on my stuff every waking moment. During the times that I have talked to individuals, I would get visions about what they would be bothered about, whether it was from ten years ago or last week. My visions would be about something that I had gone through, that they had and are going through. Since I comprehended what was going on with them I would be able to help them deal with it. The saying goes, "you cannot know what they are feeling until you walk in their shoes." I may not have walked in their shoes but I have had similar experiences as they have. I have the Lord, and my angel guides with me daily, as everyone does. I have talked with, prayed with and have asked them for knowledge, wisdom, understanding, guidance, and strength about the situation before me. I get the information in visions, such as pictures, words or a feeling. I had to learn how to interrupt what the visions had meant. As I had previously stated, I had thought that I was devil possessed for a very long time. I was constantly in prayer and I would pray that those visions would go away. Guess what? The visions became more and more and stronger. I had to keep my diaries and write them down. I had the diaries so that I did not have to keep the visions in my memory. One reason there were too many visions to remember, and if I had written them down, my guides would help me learn how to interrupt each picture and/or word and comprehend how I was to tell them to the individual before me. Also, if I would write the information down, then it would not be in my memory and the guides would immediately give me more information to comprehend. I have done that process for over twenty years and I can guarantee anyone that if you really do want to comprehend what your pictures, words or/and gut feelings mean, try it you will like it.

In July of 2004, Ted had taken me with him and we had bought a motor home. He said that I had been in that bed and bedroom for to long and I needed to get out of there. So we had bought one. We had always owned fifth wheels and our pick up truck. Then it started getting really hard for me to get in and out of the camper. One time, while I was coming out of the camper, I had blacked out and fell out of the camper. So that is one reason why I had agreed with the motor home. At that time, Cari had already met Don. I called him Mr. D. Ted, Mr. D., Cari, Mr. D.'s parents, and Alex, Cari's daughter, and Willy had emptied the fifth wheel and reloaded the motor home with everything that they had taken out of the fifth wheel. During this time, Ted, Mr. D. and his dad had moved my bed out of my bedroom and moved it to the motor home. Sharon, his mom, Cari, Willy, even little Alex had brought all the stuff from the garage to the motor home. Sharon had put it away for me. Cari and Mr. D. had stayed in the house with Willy and Alex while Ted and I had gone to Atlanta, Georgia to help his sister Barbara. Barbara had cancer for a very long time and it had been gone for a long time and then it came back. Ronda, Ted's niece, was there and so were others; however, I was glad that Ted and his sister had those weeks of being together before she had passed away. Ted and I had gone to Texas for the winter because the cold would almost kill me. In the short time that I was out of the house and in the motor home, everyone had seen a difference in me. I guess I had become more depressed staying in bed than I had realized. My body had swelled horribly; I believe one reason was because I also had to take prednisone on and off in order to deal with the pain. I went from about 140 pounds to 205 pounds in a very short time. I agreed to stay in the motor home because it was a short distance to anything that I had needed to get by for the day. My bed is in the slide out of the motor home. So when the slide out is extended, I have my own space. I had a really soft bed that on most days was great to lie down on but some days it had felt like I was lying down on cement. It is a short distance from my bed to the bathroom and from my bed to the driver's seat. By this time, I did have a motorized wheelchair; however, there was not enough room in our home to be able to use it. I had parked it outside of my bedroom door; however, it was in everyone's way. So, I basically stayed in my bed unless I had needed the bathroom facilities.

Donnie married Joni in June 2004. Her parents had saved for over a year to give their daughter a lavishing wedding. That was great if parents can afford that. They really had a very nice wedding. I had been so excited that my son was getting married; however, I did not believe that I was going to be alive to attend. You know what? I was able to be there. I was in my chair and looked swelled but I was still alive to see his great event. My son had sent me a Mother's Day card the following year after he was married that was signed, *Don and Joni.* I was very upset over that and called him and had asked him why they had sent me such a cold card. He said because I did not even give him $10.00 for his wedding. Cari had told me that I had asked Joni if it was okay to give them an IOU until after Cari had gotten married because Ted and I had no money since he was trying to make me comfortable. I had told Donnie that and I had also told him that I was lucky to even have been able to attend his wedding because I was dying. I have not heard from him again. I know that life goes on; however, I hope one day that they will come and collect the IOU that I owe while I am still alive.

It also needs to be known that their dad did not help Cari

with her wedding. I do not believe that he had helped Donnie either. For several years, Ted and I have gotten Donnie out of many money problems. His last money problem caused Ted and me a lot of money that there was little money left for Ted and I. There are many individuals that talk badly about us; however, we have helped most everyone around us that had needed and asked for the help. So why is it perhaps you may be asking that they have treated us so badly? Actually, I do not know. I have gone to prayer about it and I have come to the conclusion that I cannot make it my problem, I need to treat them how I would like to be treated and let the Lord be my strength.

Cari married Donald—Mr. D. July 10, 2004. It wasn't a very big wedding; however, it was nice and affordable. The two of them were happy and I believe they had a happy wedding day. Cari's dad showed up with his girlfriend, and my son Don and his new wife attended. They may have stayed for an hour at Cari's wedding, but I'm not sure. Mr. D.'s parents basically paid for Cari's wedding. His brother and mom did all the cooking. Ted and I helped with the decorations. That is, I was the supervisor of how the hall should be decorated. Most of Mr. D. s' family helped get the wedding together. Ted and I did not have the money to help them out because of all the tests that I had done and had to pay for.

I had felt so blessed that my daughter had included me in her wedding, even though I could barely do anything. Isn't that what families should be doing? Working together? They had gotten married at me and Ted's little church down the road from our home. Pastor Hayes had made sure that their wedding had been a success. He also had made sure that I was there able to do my part that Cari and Mr. D. When Cari walked down the isle, I cried and cried and cried just like a little baby. I was and still am so happy and proud of her.

Every time that Ted and I went south for the winter we would stop at my sister's home in Mississippi. We would stay camped in her yard for about a week or so. I thought that was great. After I had gotten sick it was a bit more difficult to go into their home, so they would most of the time come out to the camper. Jo and Larry were living in a single wide, but had decided to sell me that one and buy a double wide. She did and I had bought a mobile home from my sister, Jo, in the fall of 2004 so that Ted and I could stay in it for the winter months. About a week or so before we were going to stay in it for the winter, she let her daughter have it. Jo had paid us our deposit back; however, I wanted the trailer but Tracey had destroyed it. Since then, Jo does not really speak to me, yet, I told her that it was no big deal, so it is not the same between us. In the winter of 2005, I had e-mailed Jo that we would be near her house in March of 2006. I asked her what week would be good for us to come and visit her. She never answered me. I have to assume that we will not be going to her house.

I had believed that Jan and I were good friends. She would make me upset; however, when we would visit her, she would be involved with one of her friends and I would ask if I could help or join them. She didn't want me to join them. Jan and Rick would not come to my house anymore and we understood because Ted was retired and both of them worked. We would go there and I would help her paint or work in her garden the best that I could. I had figured that is what you do for family; you help them out when they need help. Even when they had no money, Ted and I would help. Not long after I had gotten sick and Jan had changed towards me. She had bought a very large home big enough for my bike and wheelchair, and I could get around inside her house. They had set up some 2 x 4's and a sheet of wood that leaned on top of their front stairway so I could get up and down the front outside stairs and in and out of the front door, which was great. It seems that not long after Jo and Jan had met again after many, many years, Jan and Rick could drive down to Mississippi. But no longer drive to Michigan.

In May 2006, Jan and Rick had come to my home for one night. During that time I had thought that Rick was joking with me, but instead he had gotten so angry at me. I do not know what that was about. Cari had asked me what that was all about, and I honestly had to tell her that I didn't know. She emailed me with some jokes; however, we really do not communicate with each other any more.

I had first taken study classes for my Associates Degree in 1986. I had been interested in criminal justice and had wanted to learn enough legal data to where I could protect myself from any negative people and/or situations. I had finished my Associates Degree as a paralegal. I had done my internship at a delightful facility and they had taught me many things. I felt that I learned enough information to keep me safe, but that was not what I had wanted to be when I had grown up.

I had been interested for many years to comprehend why and how individuals do some of the things that they do. I had found it quite interesting that there are so many individuals that assume that they indeed know what someone else is going to do. I, however, have learned from a very young age that you should not assume anything. You may think that someone is going do one thing; however, they actually do something else. Then what do you do? I have been talking with individuals for many years on the spiritual aspect of their lives. The Lord, Holy Spirit and my Guides have shown me so many interesting things that I have learned how to interrupt them and apply them to many of my own, as well as others, situations. I had decided to study Family Life Education and got my Bachelor of Arts Degree at

Spring Arbor College in Dearborn, Michigan in 1995–1997. There were several reasons why I had chosen the course of study. My focus for this study program was to learn how to guide and teach individuals to learn to let go of past negative memories from an educational standpoint. I had also wanted to learn how to guide these individuals from a spiritual standpoint.

One of the main reasons was to learn how the negative aspects that children learn from their parents effects them in life. I needed to learn how to talk to the children, and learn how to listen and let the children know that I do care about them without telling them how to take charge of their own situations because people do not want to be told what to do. Each individual had to realize that they were not the only ones that had gone through dysfunctional situations. My professional focus was also taken from personal experiences. My main concern was how I would acquire enough information so that I could learn how to use my own personal situations and combine it with my professional experiences to teach others, while at the same time giving them positive encouragement. Another reason was in hope to educate all individuals who have and/or had a concern about releasing yesterday's unhealthy attitudes. It seems to me that for generation after generation, people have allowed what they have learned as a child to ruin and run them today as an adult. Many individuals did not and do not know how to release the anguish that they had held and are holding onto today. It is in hope that many of those individuals will allow themselves to be guided to become positive individuals and to learn how to prevent continuous crisis of their low self-esteem. Many families have a communication barrier and it is in great hope that the void between generations will be broken and many individuals will become positive adults.

Angry

Before I had been saved I was a very angry, afraid, insecure, hateful, distrusting and a mean individual. I allowed what and how I had learned as a child run my life until 1983. I would fight my children's battles, that is, if the bullies were fighting with my kids, then I would be there to help fight for them. The last sentence is a really terrible statement. In reality, I had to learn how to guide my children to be able to take care of their own situations. As most of us need to learn you cannot fight your kids' battles because you will not be there all the time. Help guide and teach them to learn how to do it themselves. I did not trust anyone. I would start out not trusting someone, then I would get to know them fairly well and then my intuition would tell me that something was wrong, but I would start trusting them. They ripped me off or took advantage of me. It had taken me approximately one year to learn, understand and apply what the Lord was teaching me. I have forgiven everyone in my life that has hindered me. It was not easy but by the grace of God, I am on my road to succeeding. As already mentioned, I have many visions. I had to learn to hear and listen to what I was being told in the spirit. There were many days that I did not have any clue to what I was being told, yet, other days I knew and comprehended most everything. I was so amazed in what I had been seeing and learning.

I have a concern today about the many closed-minded individuals who believe that visions are not appropriate. If they do not understand, then why make negative comments? Investigate what visions are; find out what the higher power needs each one of us to be doing. If someone does not believe in God, then they must believe in something. Who do they pray to? Or who do they talk to if not talking to a person? The name *psychic* really bothers me because those individuals who are fake have tried to ruin it for God's children that really do have visions. None of the above mentioned individuals have ruined it for me though. Because I am a child of God and he has given me the visions and everything else, and only he can take it away. Everyone that helps others is and will be liable to and what they tell to others. If you know that you are not helping someone like you are suppose to, then I would suggest that you go to prayer and ask the Lord for forgiveness and ask him to show you the correct way for you to go. Have any of you that have tried very hard to *fix* others been up all night thinking about what you had said that day or several days previous?

I have found it so frustrating that there are many psychologists that immediately put a name on individuals that are having visions. Why must they jump into the situation immediately with an adverse diagnosis? I have talked with many of those individuals that have tried to figure out what is going on with them. Those people have gone to the doctor to see if they could get help comprehending what they are seeing. Please be open-minded doctors. You have had an earthly education, so now learn about the spiritual education that is available to you so that you may better assist your patients. Because of the many individual adults that do not have visions and do not comprehend what visions are about I have also had hang-ups about having visions. I am not talking about individuals that are really sick. I am talking about those individuals that have a brilliant intelligence level but other things are happening to them and they do not know who to turn to. Until recently, in 2006, I was afraid about what people would say if they knew that I had visions. That is one reason why it has taken me so long to write all this down onto paper. I have helped some *professionally known* individuals with prestige and they had wanted my name to be known. I was afraid and then I was not afraid at the time to have my name known to the public. My way of thinking was that the Lord gave me the visions; therefore, why should I be afraid. Man has a mighty nasty tongue and they say such horrible things. I have come along way with God by my side and I will stand strong with him. As stated before, spiritual warfare is around us everywhere. Spiritual warfare wants me and everyone else to be afraid and to think negative things. I ask you one and all, stay strong, and trust what you know that you know in Jesus' name.

Before and after I had entered the Family Education Program at Spring Arbor College, I talked with many people. I would cry, laugh and pray with them. I felt that the Lord wanted me to attend this program to enhance what I already knew. I know that going to this college has strengthened and confirmed the beliefs that I already had. My philosophy on life generates on many things. I know that my character traits tell a lot about me. I do intervene my character traits with how I see things from an objective, subjective, or rational view. I believe that everyone has their own points of view, and I do not intend on persuading anyone to my way of thinking. I value life personally and socially in a positive manner and I intend on guiding others to view their life in the same way. You are your own person and you need to stay that way. The only books that I have basically read are those that I had to read during my education. I read a book on Angels, four of the five Harry Potter books, and another book from Benny Hinn's writings.

In 2002, I bought a scooter because I had a problem with walking. I was not a space cadet yet, I still knew what was going on around me. I had passed out several times so the doctors thought I might have had a seizure. They put me on some horrible medicine that made me just sit in the chair where I had taken the medicine and did not go anywhere until the medicine had worn off. I think I only took a few of those pills when I had realized that something was worse going on. It was a good thing that Ted had believed me or I would have died.

I had to cut my hair very short during my illness because Ted would have to bathe me and wash my hair. He also had to feed me, which consisted of bland food and he had to cut up my stuff. If I was doing great that day I would use my one hand to eat because it was to hard to eat using a utensil. I only had my right arm to do all my stuff that I wanted to do. At first I had become so angry because I had worked so hard to get through college and get into our new home and everything else. I had great plans to decorate our new home, which I had started, but I am still working on it. I thought I was doing pretty well, but it seemed that every week I was getting worse. The summer of 2001, just before the fall, Ted and I had built the deck we now have on the south side and front of our house, and he and I had put new siding on our home with the help of my son Donnie. That was great that we have the porch and deck, because after my stroke, I needed to have Ted add a ramp onto what we had built.

In 2003 and the beginning of 2004, I basically had been bedridden. I had needed help with most of my basic necessities.

I tried not to drink to much liquid because I had a horrible time having Ted get me to the bathroom. I really do not remember very much during this time span. I had told someone once that when you go through all this pain you are a sort of a space cadet you do not realize what you are going through. However, if you go through all that pain and you are alert and know what is going around you that can be a real drag.

Food Allergies

In the fall of 2004, Ted, me, Pansy, Ted's sister, and Uncle Al (Pansy's husband) drove our motor homes to Las Vegas, Nevada where some of their family lives. We had stayed there for Thanksgiving and Christmas that year. In February 2005, we had left there and were on our way to the southern most part of Texas. The four of us had camped at the same campground until we all left at the end of March.

Not long before we had left with Pansy and Al to go to Las Vegas, Ted had bought me a laptop computer. At first, it was quite scary to use and comprehend. I had gotten use to it and could email everyone that I had an email for. In February, I was searching the Web to see if I could find anything on Fibromyalgia. I had gotten so excited because there was so much stuff on the disease and other diseases that the doctors said that I had. Even though there was a great amount of information, I still did not find any help for me as I was hoping to have found. One day, I had come across a website that a Dr. Dantini had written about his medical history. I had found it quite interesting. During my illness, I had been to over ten specialists that did not know how to help me. Am I in luck? I had read and reread his data for several days. I had told Ted, Pansy, Al, Cari, and Mr. D. about the doctor and we all agreed that I had nothing basically to loose. I had called him and his nurse set me up an appointment. One thing that was great about this site was that I could talk to him on the telephone. The bad thing about this doctor was I didn't know if he was real or a fake. I had to go with it and trust what I knew because I was dying and I really wanted to get out of this blooming bed. So, I had talked to the nurse, Sam. I was to first send him $500.00 to Dr. Dantini's office. The $500.00 was basically used for the blood tests, the shipping, and the handling of the blood tubes. After they received the money, a blood lab would send me some tubes that I needed to take to the hospital or clinic. At the clinic, someone there would gather my blood and send the vials back to the lab address. So, in February, 2005, that is exactly what I had done. I brought the vitals to the clinic and they took my blood and sent it to the lab where it took about two weeks for the test results to come back. I had talked with the doctor for a bit and he told me that I had been allergic to certain types of food and some of the chemicals that were put in the food. If I was serious about getting better, I would have to give up most of my food. I love to eat most types of food and now that same food was killing me. He let me think about it for a couple of days. At that time I was still somewhat of a space brain and had to have Ted help me with what I did everyday. I had agreed with the doctor to quit eating and drinking all my food that I loved, except for coffee, corn, pork, soy products and some vegetables. I could no longer eat any dairy products, beef, chicken, cocoa, lemons, potatoes (which included no French fries), cane sugar, wheat, bakers' yeast, grapes, grapefruits, or tea.

So now I had to give up all that food for a minimum of six

weeks until I had talked to him again. Bread is made of wheat, so I could have no sandwiches. I could not have any of my burger king cheese whoppers again. I just love mint chip ice cream. While the four of us were still in Texas, and after I had started my *do not eat certain foods program,* Ted and Pansy would spend hours at the grocery store reading labels for me. They were trying to find me food that did not include the stuff that I could not eat. They said that there was very little food out there that I could actually eat and that was already prepared. I truly believe that they were more frustrated than I was. Ted has continued looking in every store that he goes into to see if they carry any food that I can eat. He did find some non-dairy ranch dressing for me that isn't so bad. I have gotten use to eating the new foods and when I eat something that I am not suppose to it really does not taste very good. Today, I just love vanilla flavored soymilk. There are still a lot of foods that I do need to try, but it does take a little bit of push to get them into my mouth.

It was a very tough six weeks that I have ever known. I was glad that he did not take away my coffee. Actually, I was a tea drinker, so I had to get use to coffee. I do not think it took me too long to get use to it though. I basically only drank a lot of coffee when my sister Jan and Rick were together. I had gone through so many withdrawals all at once but I wanted to feel less pain. After six weeks I did start to feel better. After two months I was able to start using my left arm again. It took several months for me to do my basic personal things myself, but today I can take my own bath and dress myself. Every once in awhile I do eat a little bit of something that I am not suppose to. The pain that I get hurts so badly that I seldom cheat on my eating. Every time that I eat bread or anything that has wheat in it, which is basically everything, I get these electrical shock feelings inside my head. They make me feel off balance and I almost fall down.

After I eat regular sugar the pain is like knives stabbing into my head in several places. Some of the pain consists of stabbing in my neck, the sides and the back of it. My hips feel as if someone is literally ripping them off. My arms start hurting and I cannot use my arms.

I have lost sixty plus pounds plus since I had stopped eating the wrong foods. On my good days I am able to walk around some, sit up in a soft chair most of the day or ride my wheelchair around the yard. I did finish painting the grandkids playhouse this summer. William, Alex, Katrina, and Thackery have helped me paint and fix the playhouse. After we had finished the work, I had been stuck in bed for over a week. That really was not too bad because at least I was able to get up and do something. Even though the doctors had told me to take my medicine, and to stay warm and get ready to die, I am not ready to die until the Lord wants me to come home. Until then, I will keep working and living my life until he does.

In 2005–2006 I had taken classes online for my Masters of Education at American Intercontinental University of Georgia and finished the program with a GPA of 3.84. I almost had a 3.98 before I had taken the last class. The class was on a technological program named the Lectora Program. I had worked over and over again on that program and I believe that today, I basically know how to use that program. I do not know why, but I had the most horrible headaches during the time of taking that class. I did not cheat by eating the wrong foods, but maybe because I had been working my brain more.

This is June of 2006. I have finished my Masters of Education and thought I would check out the jobs that might be available. There are some that I am educated for; however, the ones so far that I have looked at want you to have five years experience in the position that you are applying for. So I was asking myself, should

I really go on with my education? I had wanted to go on with my education for a Doctorate of Education. First, I will see if I will be allowed to teach online after I am finished with this study program. Even though I had been terribly frightened about using a computer before I had started again with my education, I sure am glad that I had given it a try. What I actually wanted to be when I grew up was a Psychologist. However, since my Masters had been in education, I am going to continue in that field hoping that there will many individuals that I will be able to plant the seed to help them grow. So I am going to go to Walden University, online education, to get my PhD. in Higher Education.

Suggestions

There are so many reasons why individuals continue with their education. I really believe that the main reason should be to do it for you. Do not get your education because of what someone else wants you to do. I have heard that parents want their kids to go to school for what the parents want them to learn. I believe that is the reason that kids fail in school. Individuals go back to school because it will make someone else happy. Everyone needs to do things in life because *they* want to do it. Things that will improve your self worth. A good question to ask yourself is, "What do I want to be when I grow up?"

Take the basic classes that are needed to receive your Associates Degree. Hopefully, there is an adult that is available to talk to you that has your best interest in mind. Young adults do not know what they want to be when they grow up and that can lead to a mess in the lives of those young people when they do get older.

Write a list of all your favorite hobbies. What types of areas catch your interest more than sixty percent of your liking? Put that list away for a week or so, bring it out, and rewrite if you need to. What things do you enjoy doing? For example, do you like to work in the garden? Perhaps then you might want to be a decorator, or an architectural engineer. Do you like to help others? You could be a doctor, lawyer, teacher or maybe even a principal at a school or university.

The Heavenly Father seems to have a better watch over you and me after you are born again. He has always given his Angels watch over us but now we can comprehend what they are trying to tell us better. Angel Guides give us pictures and words, dreams and knowing what we know in our daily walks of life. We just have to listen and make notes to what the visions are.

We take those visions and compare them to everyday human life items and that is how we get an understanding of what they are telling us to help guide our lives. For example, say that you see a motorcycle in a vision in front of your face. Write that down on paper and time and date it. Now what does a motorcycle mean to you in your everyday waking hours? To me, because my step-brother had been killed on a motorcycle, it reminds me of someone being careless or a negative situation is about to happen. Write it down under what you just were told to write. For example, what if you see a dog? What does it mean to you? I have a little white dog and he is my baby. So, if I see little dogs in a vision, to me, it means good things will happen to whom ever. I knew of a large, mean dog. So when I see a large dog in a vision I know that something bad is going to happen.

It is so important to write down your visions so that you can use them to teach you to comprehend what your visions mean. Some of you may not have visions, but you do have a 'gut' feeling. Basically do the same thing. When you are going to say something to someone, do the words seem to disappear? If the answer is yes, then that means for you to be quiet and just listen to what you are hearing. There are so many of you that have pictures and words, but they make you afraid. Please do not be afraid. In the beginning, I do have to admit that I was petrified about all the visions that I had been given, but in time you will find out that those visions will help you in your everyday activities. The Bible does say, that dreams will be given, visions will be given, and Angels will be given watch over us. What I have learned is that every human is a spirit with blood, guts, skin and bones and etc. The Lord knew us before we were born. What a great statement, he knew us before we were born. I know that there are going to be many people that will want to *discuss* my words and I say okay, but then do you believe what you know that you know. If you do, then you will know what that statement means.

If you really think about it, my life story has basically nothing to do with those individuals in my life. Those that were in my life were allowed to be there for many reasons and only for a short time. My life has shown what had happened to me without my consent. I had allowed others to take advantage of me. As I have gotten older, I have worked diligently on using the word *no.* Ask yourself this question, who on this whole earth can you change, fix or make do anything? Oh sure, with quite a struggle you can finally have someone do something you want them to do, but how long did they do it? After you had quit yelling, screaming, fighting and/or arguing and you had become a nice person again, did they go right back to what they had been doing in the first place until you acted like a real monster, fooled you, again? There are others of you that do not use the outward approach; instead you use the inward approach. You do not say anything and you let it build up inside of you, and then your health goes down hill. So you see you actually did not make them do anything; they had control over you and had made you become a nasty individual or you had become very sick. Your job is not to save the world.

Some of you work very diligently everyday to not do things that one of your adult figures do. But you find yourself doing exactly what they are doing. Why? Because what are you concentrating on? You are concentrating on not being like them. You are concentrating not doing things like they do.

I definitely can tell you one way that will help you out because I had been given the vision many years ago after I had whipped my son for writing all over Shirley's dresser. I had worked diligently for years to not be like her, and I was becoming like her. In prayer one night I had gotten a vision about what to do, and now I will share it will all of you that are reading this because I actually have shared this with thousands of individuals already and they also have told me that it worked when they had made the commitment to use it. The word is *commitment*. I was told to find one positive or one funny thing about the individual that I was working so hard on not being like. It did take me awhile to find one thing, but I did. Shirley had the beautiful smelling fragrance that she had put into the bathwater that I got to use after the third use. Every time I had thought of Shirley, or had to talk to her I had to have her image in my brain, instead of her nastiness in my brain. I had put the nice smell of fragrance in my brain. It had taken a while to accomplish this because I was new at the game; however, it had worked. I truly believe that is the only way that I know that I have forgiven her for all the hell that she had put me and my family through. You see, I had let what she had done to me become me. What she had done to me had control over my actions. She was bitter, I was bitter. She was angry and mean; I was angry and mean.

I was saved and my Angel Guides gave me the data and I am no longer mean and angry. Bless Shirley. Robert Sr. had beaten me with 2 x 4's. Oh, I wanted to kill him. Every time I would think of him, I would get so upset and cry hysterically. My job was to not make what he had done to me make me do to my children. He had a lovely pinky ring. When I thought of him, I immediately had that ring in my vision, my memory, and thoughts and did not allow his nastiness to get into my thoughts. I concentrated on that ring forever it seemed like. I also would say the Lords' prayer over and over and over constantly every waking moment of my day. I had also said the name 'Jesus' over and over and over forever. Because if Jesus is for you, who can be against you? Yes the spiritual warfare will be against you forever; however, Jesus will love you and always be on your side giving you strength and the words that you will need to make it through any negative situation. The Holy Spirit will always be there for you after you accept him. He is a gentleman and will never hurt you.

I had learned through the years that we deal with some type of cosmic within the universe. There are experts out there that know what I am talking about probably better than I ever will. And then there are those that only pretend to know what I am talking about. Those individuals that are pretending are definitely liable for what they are talking about and what they are telling others. Since the Lord knew us before we were born, it makes sense to me that we are spirit first.

The night that my brother had passed away, we were all first at the ER and then he was brought to his room while Ted and I had sat outside down the hallway in a waiting room. Out of the corner of my eye I had seen movement. I had looked to see what it was and it was my brother Bobby in all white moving towards me. As he moved by me he stuck his tongue out at me like he always had, smiled and kept on going. I had watched him go into the wall and had been so enthralled with what I was seeing, and then I had heard my named being called by him from down the hallway. At first, I had been confused because I had just seen him go through the wall, yet, I had heard him calling me. Wow! Ted and I had gone to his room where the doctor and nurses had put him on life support. I had found out later that they had kept him that way because the doctors wanted him to be a donor.

Anyways, during the time he was on those machines, we had a cookout at our house. Ted was out there getting the grill fired up and ready to get the food cooked. Suddenly, he ran into the house and kept yelling, make him stop it, make him quit talking. I could not figure out what he had been talking about. So I had gone out to the grill where he had been outside of the garage. Ted started telling me that Bobby had been talking to him and had freaked him out. I could not hear Bobby, but I could see him. We had gotten Ted calmed down and he would tell us what Bobby was saying and I would tell them where he was standing. I cannot remember all of what he said, but it was a wonderful moment for me. Later that day, Rick had gone to the basement of my home and had flown literally immediately back up the basement stairs. When he had gotten to the main floor where we were all staring at the stairs, he was white as a ghost and his hair was standing on end. I had seen Bobby's spirit right behind Rick and Bobby said, "gotcha," and Rick and was not laughing. Of course, we were all laughing, except for Rick, at Bobby's joke towards Rick. A few days later I was in the basement washing laundry when again out of the side of my eye, I had seen something moving towards me. It startled me at first but after I had found out that it was Bobby, I did apologize to him and asked him to come back. Of course, he did and he visits me almost every day. Ted said that Bobby said that he missed me terribly and just wanted to give me a hug.

I am a vessel of the Lords. I am a messenger for him. I do not claim to have all the powers nor the answers but I do claim to know and love my God with all my heart. He uses me as his vessel and I am eager to be used by God. He has honored me with visions and I will help and guide whoever the Lord sends to me.